Street Performers in America

Passing the Hat

PATRICIA J. CAMPBELL

Photographs by Alice Belkin

DELACORTE PRESS/NEW YORK

Published by
Delacorte Press
1 Dag Hammarskjold Plaza
New York, N.Y. 10017

First printing

Designed by Giorgetta Bell McRee

Library of Congress Cataloging in Publication Data

Campbell, Patricia J. Passing the hat.

Bibliography: p.
Includes index.
1. Street theater—United States—Juvenile literature.
2. Street music and musicians—United States—Juvenile literature. I. Belkin, Alice. II. Title.
PN3203.C3   792'.0973   81–65502

ISBN 0–440–06824–X (pbk.)   AACR2
ISBN 0–440–06833–9 (lib. bdg.)

CONTENTS

Contents

FOREWORD

Perhaps you've seen them practicing their pin passes, tuning their guitars, gearing up for the evening's revels. Street performers—in your town, on your streets. There, along the avenue, in the square. They've been there for a couple of years, come to think of it.

Who are they, anyway?

Where did they come from?

Why are they out there?

What makes them do what they do?

I started on the streets when I was six. A neighborhood kid's sidewalk show for charity. My partner was eight. We did two comedy routines. Twenty years later I'm still working the concrete. Taking risks. Listening for the laughter.

It's true, we're the lowest common denominator in

1

show business, but we're proud of it. We don't need cameras, television, or commercials. We don't use spangles, glitter, or echo chambers. We don't even need a theater. We're live wire. We don't need anything but an audience. We're anti-inflationary—after all, free never goes up in price.

You've got to be good out there. You've got to be original. Among the innovators there are no two acts, no two talents, alike. Audiences don't just walk away if they don't like you—they ride, skate, drive, sometimes rudely, always before paying.

You think you've got what it takes? Go ahead, take a chance! First, spend years learning your skill. Then, learn how to handle a crowd. Be wise and wary for the children; witty and worldly for the adults. Learn compassion for drunks; patience for the teenagers standing behind you. Deal with the bus exhaust. Accept the rain. Love your failures. Conquer your mistakes. Live for praise and pennies. Can you make magic in this theater of no frills? You'll know soon enough. Your audience will tell you. They'll let you know and you'll see the results immediately. In your hat, your guitar case, whatever you use to collect your wages. It's brutal, but it's honest.

When Patty Campbell first approached me with mike in hand, I probably thought, "Here it comes. Another 'But what do you *really* do for a living?' sort of few minutes." I was prepared to be nice. The evening was cool and friendly. We were clicking that night, and after all, this intense yet soft-spoken woman may just have contributed to my salary. Certainly I had no way of gauging her true excitement and interest. After five years in the business, it seemed as if few serious reporters had bothered to notice the resurgence of street performing in their cultural midst. It wasn't long before Patty's genuine concern had my partner and me rhapsodizing on the glories of street work. We told her things about our lives, our dreams, our philosophies. She obviously had her questions down and was serious about the subject. In fact, she had spoken to, and would continue to speak with, many others in our trade for well over a year. The result of her conversations, her research, and her commitment is this book. As you read, you will follow Patty on her journeys around the country as she sought out the best in the business, following tips from passersby, reports from other performers, and responding to the call of her own flights into the spirit of the streets. Some that she met are gypsies. Some have large hometown followings. Some are there to make money on their way to something else. And some are there for the duration, a growing cadre of young professionals who see the streets as their mission, their art, and their business.

Patty has talked to them, lived with them, watched them work. She has checked out the clowns, the jugglers, the mimes, the acrobats, the puppeteers, the singers, the dancers, the comics, the magicians, the pickers, and the pluckers, always looking for what makes them tick, why they do what they do and how, who's watching and who's walking away. She has questioned them, cuddled and cajoled them. Now she reports back to you.

I think you should read this book. I'm proud to be included in its pages. Go ahead! Read! Then hit the streets. You're expected. The show is starting any minute now. . . .

AL SHAKESPEARE
Boston, Massachusetts

The author interviews Peter Damien

A FESTIVAL
IN THE STREETS

"A terrible life, but a happy one."
—Henri Murger, *Scènes de la Vie de Bohème*

New Orleans—It is Mardi Gras time, and from a table in the Café Pontalba I can see down the length of Jackson Square. A feast of color and sound fills the long cobbled space. Closest to the open French windows of the café is a saxophonist in a burgundy velvet blouse. Just beyond, a magician stands on an upended milk carton and delicately pulls a red chiffon scarf from the air. On the low stairs of the cathedral an ashen-faced mime in purple tux and top hat creates a somber parody of the scene. Farther on, a clapping, dancing group surrounds a blues guitarist; he is soon joined by a washboard player and another saxophonist. Next to them a pianist plays doggedly away at the "Minute Waltz," and above the heads of the crowd a juggler stands on his partner's shoulders and tosses clubs high into the air.

New York—The cold winter is over at last, and on this sunny Sunday in late spring all Manhattan wants to be outdoors. The path in Central Park is filled with well-dressed strollers. Up ahead at a bend a rope has been strung between two trees; on it a fiddler dances precariously while he plays a jaunty tune. In the grassy distance a Puerto Rican trio has set up huge amplifiers and has gathered an admiring crowd for their imitation of the Beatles. A chalk circle on the asphalt walk encloses a petite mime, and by the Seal Pool in the Children's Zoo an aging buffoon in a pointed hat and polka-dot knee breeches dances stiffly with a wire ring from which floats a cascade of pink and purple bubbles.

San Francisco—Along Jefferson Street in Fisherman's Wharf the midsummer tourist season is in full swing. The narrow sidewalks are cluttered with the tables of street vendors selling "handmade" jewelry from Taiwan. The breeze from the bay brings a gutter-smell of yesterday's crab shells. At an intersection the walk widens, and a circle of tourists gawks at a mime frozen in midpose beside her tip can. As they watch, her head turns slowly, her arms swing, and she glides across the pavement, feet barely skimming the ground in an eerie robot imitation. At the foot of Ghirardelli Square a stout, middle-aged black man with a guitar insults foreign visitors genially in any one of twenty languages. In the distance a camera-clicking crowd surrounds a tall canvas-covered box with a window flap out of which a wild-eyed trumpeter emerges at the drop of a coin, and up the hill by the Cannery a frock-coated pianist thumps out ragtime from a pickup truck.

Boston—Tiny lights twinkle in the trees at Quincy Market on this warm Friday evening, and at an open-air bar a gathering of conservatively dressed people are talking and laughing, letting down from the hard workweek. Near historic Faneuil Hall several hundred chortling spectators are sitting on the brick pavement, ringing two tall men who are improvising a satirical song from audience suggestions. Down the broad mall people scurry to join a crowd surrounding a flamboyant trio of jugglers whose intricate passes are accentuated by throbbing drums and cymbals. At the curb three broad-shouldered acrobats in clown makeup are unloading mats and a springboard from a van and warming up with flips and handstands as they wait their turn for performance space.

These musicians, mimes, jugglers, magicians, and madmen are buskers—a profession as old as civilization, but one that has fallen into disrepute in the United States until quite recently. The very word has almost disappeared from American speech, and we have to resort to the phrase "street performer" to describe them.

This new breed of entertainer are people who make their living by performing in the open air. They work for themselves, whenever and wherever they wish. They go out to sidewalks, plazas, malls—anyplace there is foot traffic—and find a likely spot to entertain. Into the bustle of pedestrians they cast their talent, whatever that may be, and try to charm the passerby into stopping to watch and, at the right moment, into feeling that payment is due for pleasure received. The street performer must contend with traffic noise, with wind and cold and heat, with apathy from the public and hostility from merchants and police. But when all is going well, the sun is shining, the audience is laughing and clapping, and the money rains down at the end of the act, there is no other form of show business so satisfying and so adventurous.

Who are these people, and why are they willing to forsake the security of a steady job for the free and risky existence of the streets? How is it they have the audacity, the foolhardiness—and the courage—to dispense with life insurance, VISA, car payments, neckties, and retirement plans? As show business people how can they do without agents, advertising, and reviews? What kind of person is willing to give up the American Way of Life and to go out into the street with only his bare talent and create a theater experience reduced to its minimum essentials—a performer and an audience?

In the late summer of 1979 I set out to find some answers to these questions. As a longtime resident of bohemian Venice Beach, California, I had always numbered street performers among my friends and had danced for money in the streets myself at fairs and festivals. To gain some insights into the meaning of this new people's theater, photographer-psychologist Alice Belkin and I went traveling to major urban centers in the United States. I talked with hundreds of performers in five cities—squatting on curbs, leaning against shop windows, or sitting on stairs of public buildings, visiting them in elegant town houses or seedy apartments, rapping with them late into the night in fashionable bars or shabby coffeehouses. And I soon found myself accepted into the underground network, an admirer and friend. In exchange for the loss of objectivity, I gained understanding of the fierce need for freedom that runs through all these divergent lives. For like the jongleurs of the Middle Ages they have found a way to exist outside the structures and pressures of their society.

The history of busking is the history of urban civilization. There have been street performers at least as long as there have been streets. But because such entertainers were beneath polite notice, their existence was seldom documented in serious literature, and we have to infer the teeming theatrical life of the streets from oblique mentions, occasional pictures, and the mark their passing has left on language ("charlatan," which originally meant "one who draws a crowd," or "mountebank"—"he who climbs up on a bench").

In Wickham Boyle's directory of New York street performers titled *On the Streets*, Richard Bruno has listed some of these traces.

> There is an illustration of an ancient Egyptian street performance, complete with the performer's colleague passing the hat among the spectators. The Greek historian Xenophon describes a dinner, at which one of the guests was Socrates, that culminated in an acrobatic and mime display by two performers from Syracuse. Close cousins of the Greek mimes were the Phylakes, who traveled performing their bawdy farces on portable wooden stages and always included much acrobatics in their presentations. The mimes, with much of Grecian culture, moved to Italy and mixed with an indigenous theatre form, the fabula atellana, to eventually produce the comedies of Plautus and Terrence. . . . With the growing antipathy of the Church for the theatre, legitimate drama in Rome declined, and in the sixth century, the emperor Justinian, whose wife, Theodora, was an ex-mime herself, closed the theatres. For the next 500 years, street performers were the sole perpetrators of theatrical activity in Europe.

These itinerant entertainers of the Middle Ages were known as jongleurs, troubadours, minstrels, gleemen. Their versatility was amazing. They could sing, play an instrument (usually the fiddle), dance, tumble, juggle, tell stories, conjure—and sometimes they even traveled with a trained bear. The common folk loved them and welcomed the glimpse of magic they brought to their grim lives, but the nobles feared such free spirits and regularly persecuted, jailed, and burned them—although they first chose the best for their own households.

In England village fairs were great gathering places for jongleurs (in exactly the same way that many modern street performers also often work the Renaissance Faire circuit). The sheer numbers of entertainers these festivals attracted is shown by an anecdote from the year 1212. The Earl of Chester was being besieged in his castle by the Welsh. He sent word to his henchman Roger de Lacy, the constable of Chester, to send reinforcements. The annual fair of the city was then in progress, so Lacy rounded up all the jongleurs and marched them off to save the earl. When they appeared in the distance, presumably juggling as they came, the Welsh retreated in hasty confusion.

Throughout the later Middle Ages and the Renaissance there are repeated references to street entertainers, flowering with the development in Italy in the sixteenth century of the commedia dell'arte, from which our modern clowns and mimes both are descended. The tradition has continued unbroken in Europe to the present day, with such rich regional variations as the Pearly kings and queens of London.

In the United States the tradition was transformed in ways suitable to the psychology and distances of a new nation. The revolutionary spirit inspired a flood of political ballads, printed on large sheets called "broadsides" and hawked in New England towns by streetsingers. Ben Franklin himself sold his printer's wares by singing on corners. As the nation expanded westward, buskers followed in the form of the Mississippi showboat, the minstrel show, the small traveling circuses with their torchlight parades and calliopes, and the fast-talking medicine-show huckster.

With the urbanization of America, more European forms of busking began to appear on the city streets, and the waves of immigration of the late nineteenth century made German bands and Italian hurdy-gurdies a commonplace in New York. Streetsinger Stephen Baird, who is the national authority on the history of busking, pointed out that as late as 1923 the license department of that city reported eight hundred organ grinders and an equal number of other itinerant street musicians. In the poorer neighborhoods, vocalists took advantage of the good acoustics in the courtyards of tenements by singing with guitar, mandolin, or violin. The housewives showed their gratitude by showering the singer with paper-wrapped coins flung from their windows above. But with the coming of electronic entertainment in radio and movies, such street music began to seem old-fashioned and naïve, and on January 1, 1936, Mayor Fiorello La Guardia signed its death warrant by canceling the license structure, explaining that the city should no longer go into partnership "in this concession of mendicancy." For a time vaudeville continued to fulfill the function of people's theater, but when it too died, a generation grew up without ever seeing a live entertainer.

By 1940 the street musician had become an object of pity and disgust. Only those who were truly desperate resorted to trying to earn a few pennies in the street. The legless, the armless, the blind or hopelessly maimed, would persuade a merchant to tolerate their presence at the door, and there they would saw away tunelessly at a cracked violin or squeeze doleful melodies from a shabby accordion, completely devoid of hope and talent. With casual cruelty people passing by would avert their eyes or drop a few coins in the cup and hurry on as quickly as possible. Such performances were little better than elaborate forms of begging.

But in the late fifties young people in revolt began to take to the streets, congregating in great numbers in the Haight-Ashbury district of San Francisco, in Greenwich Village in New York, and in other centers of social protest. Most were homeless, penniless, and jobless. And many of them had guitars slung over their shoulders, for the folk-song revival of the early fifties had spawned a whole new generation of amateur musicians. What could be more natural than that they should play for each other in parks and on street corners, and that when a crowd gathered, they should pass a grimy hat for the cost of some food and a night's lodging? By the end of the sixties America had taken to the streets by the thousands to protest the Vietnam War, and happenings and guerrilla theater built public acceptance and expectation of drama and color around the next corner. From these roots evolved a new generation of skillful and imaginative performers who found in the streets that place to be bad that disappeared with vaudeville, a free theater in which to hone their acts and to develop their talents.

Other than the love of freedom there are no common characteristics of personality, background, or life-style that describe the average street performer. Men in their late twenties and early thirties predominate, but my interviewees ranged from five to seventy-five years old, and there were a number of women among them. Some performers have never worked the streets anywhere but in their home cities. Others wander the whole country or travel a consistent circuit between two or three cities. A few live out of a backpack, crashing wherever they can, and even sleeping beside the road when luck gives out. Others live in their cars or in vans fitted out for a gypsy existence, or have comfortable apartments or own luxurious homes in good neighborhoods. Some have grown up in the life as waifs surviving by their talents. Others have chosen to drop into it from flourishing careers in law or medicine or teaching. Still others are actors and musicians waiting for the big break. A surprising number are college graduates, but some have almost no formal education. Some work only when the spirit or the landlord moves them. Others follow a rigid schedule. Not all love the street—a few spoke bitterly of their life as outcasts. Not all are committed to it for life or make their whole living from it. But in every city I visited I found a hard core of people who had dedicated their lives to the street, who saw themselves as bearers of a tradition, and who were articulate and thoughtful about their place in the world.

———————————————●———————————————

STU BUCK'S WORKING DAY

A balmy evening in New Orleans and Stu Buck is on his way to work, his big flat autoharp case in one hand and his little pig-nose amplifier slung over the other shoulder by a twisted rope. I tag along to watch. First stop is at the foot of Jackson Square on Decatur Street. Stu sets up next to a concrete planter, between a row of shops and the promenade. He opens the case and lovingly lifts up the autoharp, tucks it under his arm. Then with one hand he gathers up the little red and white packages of extra strings and piles them out of sight behind the open case, drops in a dollar bill and a few coins to prime the pot. He sets out the amp and plugs it into the harp, tries a few chords, and is off into his first number, belting out

"Jambalaya" in his clear baritone into the empty air.
". . . Jambalaya and a crawfish pie and fillet gumbo . . .
Son of a gun, we'll have big fun on the bayou!" A couple
of people stop tentatively. At the end of the song there is
a scatter of applause; Stu bows. "Thank you very much,
ladies and gentlemen; welcome to the Stu Buck show!"
But it is too soon; they drift off, embarrassed. Stu
launches into another song, cradling the autoharp up
against his ear and bending over it in a bouncing, shuf-
fling dance. More people stop to listen; a young couple
with big paper cups of beer in hand sing raucously, people dance a bit. A few quarters smack into the case. Stu
plays fast and loud, keeping the energy up, and at the
end of the set there are dollar bills among the change.
"Thank you, thank you . . ." but the street is empty again.
Catching his breath, he sweeps the strings with a silvery
sound and starts a quieter tune. Above on the balcony
two women lean over, glasses in hand. "Hey, that's
pretty!" says one. Stu milks it, leaning back to smile at
them and ending with a flashy cadenza, and they throw
money down, missing the case. He picks it up, blows
them a kiss. Now it's time to move on. "I wonder if I
could make it across the street by the Café du Monde?"
he muses. "I got chased there last week . . . Well, come
on, we'll try it." The corner proves to be a good spot,
and before he has played three energetic tunes a crowd
of thirty people is singing and dancing. I join in; the
rhythm is irresistible. An elderly couple appears, holding hands, and Stu, with a polished instinct, begins the
"Tennessee Waltz." Sure enough, they embrace and
dance, a slow cheek-to-cheek circling, to cheers and
clapping. Afterward they thank Stu and explain that they
are in New Orleans on a second honeymoon. When
they leave, he turns to me. "Now that's what makes it
all worthwhile," he says with satisfaction. "Jambalaya"

Stu Buck in the
French Quarter

once more, and then he packs up and moves on in an almost superstitious search for the perfect spot. We wander down Royal Street and try several places ("Do you think there's enough light here? Or is it better across the street?"). Every number Stu plays full out, high energy, dancing and giving totally of himself even when nobody listens, when people walk past without even glancing his way. Once two teen-age boys in Western hats skirt the circle and snort, "That sucks!" Sometimes people sling change into the case as they pass by; groups form and disperse. " 'Cause tonight I'm gonna see my ma cher amio . . . Son of a gun, we'll have big fun on the bayou!" A friend happens by, joins in harmony on a song. He has been at it for four hours now; my legs ache from standing. Stu's voice is growing hoarse; I go in search of a bar and bring him back a beer. When I return, he is playing "Cielito Lindo" for a delighted couple from Mexico, who exchange a few words of Spanish with him and leave a three-dollar tip. Other spots, more tunes. Always loud, up, bouncy. At last Stu squats to count the money after another hour. "Twenty-five fifty," he says, pocketing it. "Not too bad." He snaps the case shut and hefts the pig-nose to his shoulder wearily. "Come on, babes, let's go home. I've jambled my last laya for tonight."

THE GOOD PLACES

Street performing in the United States is centered in four cities—San Francisco, New York, Boston, and New Orleans. A few other towns—Philadelphia, Seattle, Key West, Los Angeles—and some college communities— Berkeley, Boulder, Austin, Cambridge—allow some limited busking. The phenomenon is spreading to more towns each summer, but it is the big four that are home base, nurturing place, and big time for street performers. Each of these places has its own pattern for the entertainer, its own ambiences and seasonal and diurnal rhythms, and each fosters its own style of sidewalk theater, its own style of audience reaction, and its own style of police harassment.

The parts of town where buskers congregate are highly specific. You may see dozens of performers for five blocks, and then, across the street and farther on, none. Ever. This segregation of street entertainment reflects not only the density and receptivity of pedestrian traffic but an uneasy mental map of truce between performers and civic authorities. The good places within each city are part of the folklore of the road for performers, and tales of comparison are part of every encounter between traveling entertainers.

The very best of the good places is San Francisco—but only for those who are already there. Modern American street performing began twelve years ago in San Francisco (although some New Yorkers may disagree), and many of those pioneers are still on the streets with shows honed to perfection by years of audience correction. "San Francisco acts are more colorful, more interesting, more theatrical. The showmanship is superior," says Suggs the Mime, herself one of the pioneers. To that description I would add one word—*bizarre*. For there is an edge of nuttiness to many of the most successful Bay Area street shows— Hokum Jeebs playing the can-can to a cacophony of dozens of clattering mechanical false teeth; Sister Mary San Andreas tap-dancing in a nun's habit; juggler Mike Davis spewing chewed apple and raw egg down his ruffled shirt front; that Baghdad-by-the-Bay landmark, the Human Jukebox . . . .

Perhaps this quality is a result of San Francisco's traditional toleration for eccentricity, but more likely it has developed as performers have attempted to catch the attention of tourists jostled on narrow walks and assaulted by all the competing colors, flavors, and smells of Fisherman's Wharf. For the Wharf is where it's at (although an occasional busker risks downtown Union Square or even Market Street), and the audience is primarily out-of-towners come to see the sights.

The temperate climate gives the Bay Area a powerful advantage over other cities in the eyes of outdoor performers: "It's the only place in the United States really that you can work all year long and still survive," they claim. Strong ocean winds and damp fogs are only occasional deterrents. The tourist season in San Francisco knows no end, although it does wax and wane, and since tourists know no workdays, the energetic performer can make hay on the street seven days a week whether the sun shines or not.

For these reasons many San Francisco performers are firmly entrenched long-time residents or natives, and have never worked the streets of any other city. A hard core of Old Boys (and Girls) dominates the scene and monopolizes the best spots, and newcomers can be given a very hard time. Anna Fessenden, a member of a charming string group called Allegra, recalls trying to break into the action: "We played there for three days and got moved around a lot by other performers. They'd snarl, 'I've had this spot for fifteen years—now move it!' "

However, I also saw examples of cooperation and support among performers, an attitude that is far more typical of the whole fraternity of street entertainers. Classical guitarist Don Gribble described how a system was worked out for sharing the choice territory of the cable car turnaround. This spot is an ideal location, because lines of tourists wait there all day long; every ten minutes, when the car pulls clanging in, they file past a collection point and a new captive audience is produced. Performers were arriving at night with sleeping bags, then playing the next day to the point of total exhaustion before giving up the spot. "We realized nobody was winning," said Gribble, so the competitors met and worked out a schedule of two- and three-hour segments.

The mild weather, the streams of tourists, and the carnival atmosphere at the Wharf make San Francisco attractive to street performers, but the unique development of

that city's street scene is the stages that book buskers and allow them to pass the hat to a seated audience in a protected environment. There are three of these at the Wharf: the Cannery, Ghirardelli Square, and Pier 39. Each is part of a complex of shops and restaurants, and each auditions and books performers months ahead.

The Cannery is a rambling four-story building that used to be a fish canning factory, until some clever entrepreneur got the bright idea of gutting it and converting the brick passages and courtyards into shops and restaurants and bars. An inner patio filled with trees and vines has become a small outdoor theater with a little stage surrounded by benches and picnic tables for the nearby lunch stalls and cafés. Here a street performer can work to a seated audience in a relaxed mood and be safe from wind, noise, drunks, and police. A second performance area is the Alcove under an archway at one of the entrances, where guitarists or small instrumental groups play.

Paul Levey, who is in charge of the booking for the Cannery, sees himself as entertainment middleman. "I'm here to protect the middle-class sensibilities," said Levey, himself an Old Boy who has a long history of street performance with a Dixieland band, the Bourbon Street Irregulars. "I'm here to keep the winos from playing in the Cannery. I'm a liaison between the shopkeepers and the street people. When I audition I no longer look for talent; I no longer look for originality—I look for people who are neatly dressed and who don't look like they'll be drinking wine or smoking dope in public—that's primarily what I look for," he said fiercely.

"You'd be surprised at some of the people who have come and gone," Paul said—Robin Williams, for instance, or Shields and Yarnell. "There's no mistaking a good act. During the audition even the shopkeepers come out of their stores to see what this is."

Although merchants can have aesthetic appreciation for a good street performance, when it comes to business they are hostile and afraid that the buskers will drain customers and dollars away from their shops—an antagonism I was to find all over the country. In deference to this paranoia toward street performers acts are scheduled only every other half-hour at the Cannery. Performers who have been given a three-hour segment can play on the hour until half past, and then they must sit and wait for thirty minutes to allow time for the crowd to disperse, presumably to the shops.

Paul feels that street performing has reached a point of saturation now in San Francisco—far too many guitarists and jugglers—and that the Golden Age was 1973, when $200 and $300 days were not unusual. Nowadays the average take for a good afternoon in the Cannery is about $100 (as contrasted with $50 to $60 on the street). He books six to eight weeks ahead, and turns away more people than he accepts during the summer months. Like the other entertainment directors at the Wharf, he gets frequent calls from television and film people, "but they're not really looking for talent," he complains. "What they want are freak shows—a gorilla playing the trumpet."

A few blocks down, Ghirardelli Square has classier shops, more expensive restaurants, and a generally snootier atmosphere. It too is a former factory, and the smell of chocolate still lingers on the lower floors. The main performance area is in one corner of a bare concrete plaza and lacks the coziness of the Cannery, although it is possible to draw an audience of several hundred there. Marsha Monro, the Director of Advertising and Public Relations, is in charge of entertainment. As a native San Franciscan, she is philosophically committed to street performing, and grew up with Ghirardelli Square. "I used to come here with my high school dates and walk through the Plaza and hold hands and all that. I'm a third-generation San Franciscan, and I have grown up to understand what street performing is all about and how it adds tremendously to the ambience of the city. There is such marvelous talent around—you can't imagine!" Marsha requires a letter of introduction, a resumé, and a cassette tape before she will audition a new act. She schedules far in advance—as much as four months, which would seem to weed out itinerants and other more spontaneous talent. Like Paul Levey, Marsha is in the middle of merchant-performer antagonisms: "I have to be very, very careful in the time allotments [twenty minutes on, twenty minutes off] to keep the crowd flowing so I don't disturb the business transactions."

The third street-performing stage at Fisherman's Wharf

is at Pier 39, a new development built out over the water, where there are a number of restaurants, a collection of tourist shops, a carousel, and a diving show. The atmosphere is circus, and the crowds are predominantly young families. "The Pier feels like a carnival to the crowd. The only kind of an act that works with them is a real aggressive thing," says juggler Kit Trueblood. A performer working either of the two stages at the Pier has to stop the passing crowd in mid-step and surmount the noise from carousel and calliope. Spectacular jugglers are to be seen there, and some of the best of the city's street magicians. Booking at Pier 39 is done by Rob Nelson, the Butterfly Man, himself an outstanding comedian and juggler.

Some performers are philosophically opposed to the stages of San Francisco. New York funambulist Philippe Petit said, in an article in *The Village Voice*, "In San Francisco, there is an enclosed garden where, after an audition, you are given a permit with a seal of approval and a chunk of concrete. Entertain the pedestrian from 10:38 to 2:42 P.M.! Soon they will build a roof to protect these festivities from the maritime breeze; then there will be left only the construction of a gate, the posting of an admission fee, and the street will be dead." Mindreader Glenn Gazin is even more negative: "If I'm going to book myself, I want to be paid. I think it's so ridiculous to *grovel* for the privilege of performing gratis. It's sheer exploitation."

"San Francisco loves their street artists!" says Suggs the Mime, yet unfortunately nobody seems to have convinced the police of that. It is ironic that, among the five cities I visited, the performer runs the highest risk of being arrested in the city that talks the most of supporting street theater. I was told of arbitrary busts and raids and sweeps. Everyone agreed that the situation now is not as bad as it used to be, but almost every San Francisco performer I interviewed who had been at it for more than two years had spent at least one night in jail. In other cities the police are prone to warn or threaten; in San Francisco they are more likely to pull up the Black Maria and whisk the busker off to the slammer in mid-performance.

In contrast to San Francisco's tourist sideshow, New York has a variety of street performing environments, each with its own character and audience. Central Park on weekends, Greenwich Village on warm evenings, Fifth and Sixth avenues on weekdays, Lincoln Center and Broadway before and after performances and during intermissions, the Metropolitan Museum steps, the Staten Island Ferry, and the Financial District all have regulars and aficionados.

New York pedestrians can be cold and tough, but they also know a good show when they see it. "If you can stop New Yorkers, you can really hold them," says Anna Fessenden. They are very aware of street performers and have accepted them as a legitimate part of the street scene. This is reflected in the frequent media coverage: Howard Smith often writes about buskers in his "Scenes" column in *The Village Voice*, and street stars appear on TV talk shows with regularity. Violinist Richard Wexler has even been reviewed by music critic Harold Schonberg. Wickham Boyle, the former Director of Special Projects for the New York City Department of Cultural Affairs, was given a grant from the National Endowment for the Arts to compile a directory of the city's buskers. She spent over a year "stalking the wild street performer"; her book—*On the Streets: A Guide to New York City's Buskers*—lists addresses and short descriptions of 125 performers, a small sample of the rich variety of entertainment available on the streets of Manhattan.

These streets, however, are not for amateurs or sissies. There is bad craziness out there, says ventriloquist David

24

Strassman. "The streets of New York are a zoo. In Central Park one Sunday this woman who spoke Spanish started yelling at me during the act. I guess she was drunk. Next thing I knew she came up behind me and started choking me, right in the middle of the act with the audience standing there—they started laughing, so I kind of laughed, but I couldn't *breathe*! I guess she wanted to see if I could talk without moving my lungs. So I elbowed her in the chest; she moved away and started swearing at me in Spanish. I ended the show real fast and got out of there."

The busking season in Manhattan is limited to the warm weather days of late May through October—most performers give 62 degrees as their bottom working temperature. Consequently a resident street performer must have another string to his bow to survive the winter. A very few tough it out, continuing to stand on snowy street corners like the Little Match Girl, but most eke out the cold months by finding what work they can in nightclubs and little theaters or by taking jobs as typists or busboys. Almost none, strangely enough, immigrate to the streets of warmer cities. Nor is New York a favored stop on the circuit for itinerant buskers. Many will do a few days in the Big Apple, just to say they did, but a long haul there takes a special kind of hardiness.

The New York police are surprisingly lenient with buskers, probably because they have more serious matters to worry about. Although they often ask performers to move on, they usually do it tactfully, coming up and saying quietly, "This will be the last number." Because their style is so discreet, many New Yorkers maintain that the police never bother street performers in *their* city. Arrests are rare, although not unheard of. Sometimes they even apologize for acting on a complaint.

The Central Park area is the happiest busking scene in Manhattan because strollers in the park are at leisure and in a mood to be amused. The walk to the zoo that parallels Fifth Avenue is especially nice for children, and a likely place to find mimes and clowns. The Grand Army Plaza at the foot of the park and the statues along Literary Walk are other good Central Park spots.

Greenwich Village, when the locals come out to walk on nice summer nights, is another kind of scene—colorful, intellectual, but often weird or raunchy. The action centers around Washington Square and Sheridan Square, although performers can be found on almost any of the narrow, winding avenues. The upstairs residents are often unfriendly to the noise below. "They'll call up within five minutes when you start playing," said the members of the Color by Number String Band. "Sometimes they'll call up even before you take the instrument out—they're at the windows waiting. Three of us were playing in the Village once and somebody dumped a bucket of water on us out the window." Washington Square is more hospitable; some outstanding acts—Victor Brady the steel pianist, comedian Charlie Barnett—have developed their art there.

Midday on Fifth and Sixth avenues from the Forties up to Central Park is a musical feast. The audience are office workers on their lunch or coffee breaks, and they are connoisseurs of the street scene. Classical musicians in particular find a patient and perceptive public here. On Sixth Avenue I watched five young people who call themselves the Olympic Brass Quintet puffing away at a selection from Bach's "The Art of Fugue" while a ring of twenty or thirty listeners stood quietly enjoying the difficult, demanding music. This group has been together on the street for two years, but other classical musicians can be what buskers snidely refer to as "Juilliard lunch money" —music students who are picking up a bit of change as a lark. Other types of music on Fifth Avenue range from jazz to opera a cappella to bluegrass. Irish music and pipers are especially likely to be found in the high Forties, where there are several Irish bars.

Theatergoers emerging from the first act at Lincoln Center or on Broadway sometimes are met by street performers, and there are a few buskers who specialize in this environment. The Metropolitan Museum steps are another very special place. Paul Dion, a superb mime who has performed in the streets of most of the cities of Europe, considers it one of the best spots in the world. On Sunday the site is packed with people walking back and forth on the broad sidewalk, and the steps, on which as many as a thousand spectators can sit, make it a built-in theater. Competition is fierce for the five or six spaces, and not always friendly. Paul is a regular there, but on the Sunday I watched him a bluegrass group attempted to supplant him by boldly moving into his territory during his act.

The city issues permits to buskers to play on the Staten Island Ferry. This environment, although it can be joyless, has the advantages of a seated captive audience, a structured collection time, and a shelter from the weather. However, performers are only allowed to play the ferry once a month, and the permit is no guarantee of a hassle-free performance—the boat people sometimes invoke the fine print that forbids solicitation of money. For these reasons most performers don't bother with official permission: they simply work the ferry until they are caught and told to leave.

The Financial District around Wall Street has its own flavor for performers. Puppeteer Gary Schnell enjoys surprising office workers: "The people who work in the city appreciate it a lot more than tourists. They're a responsive audience—you don't get dead crowds downtown. They go 'Oh, far out! Something's happening! All right! A performer came down here to entertain us!' " Other buskers find that while Wall Street junior executives will watch with obvious enjoyment, they are reluctant to step up and put money in the hat, perhaps feeling that something that looks like so much fun is not real work worth rewarding with cold cash.

AN INTERVIEW REFUSED

Alice smells it first—white gasoline and fire—and up ahead we see the flame leap up from a torch held low to the broken sidewalk. Against a graffiti-scarred fence a tall, awkward young man is attempting to juggle fire. This street on the edge of Greenwich Village is not a good place for a show (too much automobile traffic and almost no pedestrians) and we are curious to see him here. We stop to watch. He fails to keep the torches lit, and soon he switches to the cigar boxes. These go no better; he drops continually with loud clatterings, and his muttered attempts at patter embarrass the few spectators into leaving. The balls are a final fiasco: they leap away out of his fumbling hands and one rolls across the street so that he has to call over to have it thrown back. A man slings a quarter into the tip can without looking at the juggler and hurries away. I know this is a bad moment, but I have seen no other jugglers in New York, so I approach him. "How long have I been on the street?" he says, his eyes darting sideways. "This is my first time. And no, I don't think I want to be interviewed for a book." I see that there are little beads of sweat on his upper lip, even though the night is chilly.

A bagpiper warms up at Quincy Market

Boston is the Emerald City for street performers. A good act in a prime spot at Quincy Market can make $350 in an afternoon. The police are genial because the city has a licensing system that makes it theoretically okay to perform anywhere. The public is curious and friendly, albeit a bit unaware, and there is a strong tradition of Yankee individualism that supports self-expression—within proper Bostonian limits of propriety.

Two very unlike people have been responsible for making Boston such a promised land for street performers: developer James Rouse and streetsinger Stephen Baird.

Five years ago the waterfront area around historic Faneuil Hall in downtown Boston was a dingy collection of old warehouses and a shabby weekly flea market—all that remained of the hundred-year-old Quincy Market tradition. Then the area was discovered by James Rouse, whose Rouse Development Company has had an extraordinary track record in revitalizing declining American cities. Rouse assessed needs in Boston: "We determined a yearning for festivals and city fairs. People wanted a sense of playfulness and delight. When we saw the Faneuil Hall location—near City Hall and the waterfront, near apartments being renovated—we said 'This is it!' Our decision was greeted with massive disbelief by bankers and merchants." But Rouse's instincts were correct, and now the three long buildings with their shops and restaurants and take-out food stalls get more visitors daily than Disneyland. Although street performers were not part of Rouse's plan, the festive atmosphere of the two wide cobbled malls have proven to be an ideal background for some of the best informal outdoor theater in America.

Stephen Baird, who appeared in the previous chapter in his role as historian, has been almost single-handedly responsible for opening the streets of Boston to an official acceptance of busking. Born in Cambridge, he was schooled as a chemical engineer and turned troubadour in 1972. In that year there were only four or five other musicians regularly playing the sidewalks of the city, and they had to deal with constant police harassment. Stephen heard of a half-forgotten law passed in 1878 that allowed the licensing of street performers, and, with instincts sharpened by his years of college antiwar activity, he tracked it down through the labyrinth of city government. An audition was required, so, with dulcimer in hand, he went down to the Police Department and applied. "What's wrong with you?" they asked, revealing the link in their minds between busking and physical handicaps. Reassuring them as to his mental and physical health, he played the finale from Beethoven's Ninth on his dulcimer, encored with an Irish drinking song, paid ten dollars, and was awarded his license. However, he soon found that the permission given was for only a few square blocks of the inner city and did not allow him to receive payment for his performance. The harassment continued. Stephen launched a letter-writing campaign, threatened to sue, and, with the help of the Assistant District Attorney, succeeded in May 1973 in getting the law changed to read: "Licensee permitted to receive voluntary donations but is not permitted to solicit." The open guitar case had become legal, a situation that existed in no other major city in the United States. "Then it was a matter of educating all the cops on the beat as to the change in the law," said Stephen. It took three years, but the goal was accomplished, and today Boston is a peaceful place for street performers.

For ten dollars a year the Boston Itinerant Musician's License allows a musician to play on any public street in Boston (the Common and other parks are under separate jurisdiction). Amplifiers are permitted if the sound is not audible more than three hundred feet away. The police do a record check for felonies on applicants, although I was told that they are inclined to blink at arrest records for soliciting or street performing itself. Flaws in the license structure are that nonmusical acts are not covered (although they are not specifically prohibited either) and that the fee for musical groups of more than two players—five dollars a day—is prohibitive. Ironically enough, a recent Massachusetts State Supreme Court decision (which will be discussed in a later chapter) has probably thrown the Boston license into question by equating street performing with free speech, which cannot be limited or regulated by law. But in the long run the importance of the license structure has been to educate the public and the police to an acceptance of busking.

The effect of this civic permission has been a flourishing of street theater unequaled in any other place in the United States. Boston performers are easy in their minds. Without the need to keep a constant watch over their shoulders for the police, they have developed large, well-rehearsed groups that have a stable commitment to each other and to the streets. Without the need to be portable enough to pick up and run, they can invest in equipment, backdrops, more and better effects. On the wide-open plazas and squares and malls they can encourage their audiences to be seated and watch their longer, more relaxed and elaborate shows. Four of the most spectacular busking groups in the country—the Locomotion Vaudeville, the Slap Happys, the Fantasy Jugglers, and the Shakespeare Brothers—call Boston home. Stephen Baird's few harried colleagues in 1972 have grown into a talent pool of nearly three hundred buskers.

Harvard Square in nearby Cambridge has also played a significant role in this flowering. In 1976 the performers organized to fight for legalization, and at a victorious Council meeting Mayor Valucci defended busking by declaring: "They do it on every street corner in Italy!" Now even the Harvard Businessmen's Association is amenable. They have come to see the relationship between the crowds that fill the Square and their shops on summer evenings and the performers that those crowds have come to see. For the Harvard audience has continuity. An educated—although not necessarily an academic—crowd, they come in family groups week after week to watch their favorites and to spend an entire evening strolling from group to group. Two large traffic islands and a plaza corner are prime spots, and deep entrances to shops provide other performing alcoves after closing time. When the hat is passed, it is said that fifty percent of the audience will contribute, as compared to ten percent or less in other places. To please this discerning and appreciative public, the best troupes have developed two or three entirely different shows and have worked out a cooperative plan for utilizing the choice performing spots by turns to avoid conflicting attractions. They feel an affection for the scene there, even though it is not as lucrative as Quincy Market:

"Harvard Square is home base for us," says Al Shakespeare; "Quincy Market is just where we make our money."

Because Quincy is so profitable for buskers, the person who does the booking there wields a great deal of power. In the past the position has been the focus of some stormy sessions between performers and management. The current Community Relations Director, Phyllis Cahaly, is a young woman who tries hard to be responsive to the economic needs of performers while she treads carefully around the apprehensions of the merchants. There are two performance areas at the Market, and Phyllis tries to parcel them out so that each group gets at least four two-hour bookings a month. A new busker in town must fill out a biography card and give references and then wait up to two months to get on the roster. Phyllis in effect fills the role of central casting agent for Boston street performers; she makes dozens of referrals every week for parties, fairs, television spots.

————————————•————————————

THE FANTASY JUGGLERS AT WORK

Conga drums, snare drums, cymbals on stands, racks of clubs and balls—jugglers Don and Lana Reed and Rawd Holbrook and drummer Tom Clark are setting up at one end of Quincy Market. Already there are people waiting expectantly on benches and curbs, and more arriving all the time. Alice squirms through to crouch with her camera in the front row as the drums begin.

Lana is dancing with a parasol and a big ball. Her compact, athletic body is beautiful in a leotard, and she moves in long swooping circles while the parasol spins and dips, and on top of it the ball spins its own dance, perfectly balanced. A lyrical opening, followed by a comic turn—Rawd jumps out with a set of balls flying; they leap from his hands in controlled circles, bounce off his head, jet straight up, to his open-mouthed astonishment, while the drums underscore the comedy with tag lines of percussion. The other two join him, and then Don comes forward and crouches down with outstretched hands filled with balls. The music sinks to a quiet, persistent silvery shimmer of cymbals, and the balls revolve eerily, rotating and changing places on his palms. He turns his hands over and the balls drip down one by one, roll quickly across to the other hand, and hop back up by themselves in an uncanny circling. The small, intense moment ends, and they all three leap into the next movement of this precisely choreographed juggling suite, the drums always exactly mirroring the flight of clubs and balls, the syncopated patterns in the air. Astonishment follows astonishment, and at last the air is filled with a storm of clubs flung faster and faster between Don and Lana. Tall, ungainly Rawd swoops about interfering, seizing a club out of flight and flinging it seemingly at random back into the pattern, ducking to pick up a fallen piece as a club whizzes by his ear, and finally leaping straight up with his long legs spread, through the air thick with clubs that never touch him. The drums pound to a climax; the jugglers gather in the clubs from the air. They come forward with three long steps, arms spread triumphantly, and bow to cheers and applause as Lana spins a basket on one finger and sets it down in the middle of the space so recently filled with amazement.

If Boston is the Emerald City for street performers, New Orleans is Hometown. No other place has such a close camaraderie among buskers. Everybody knows who's in town, who got busted, who had a fight with his wife, what new acts just blew in. Performers watch each other at work with interest, sometimes even throwing quarters. They share living and performing space, have their own cafés and hangouts. Performers come and go because New Orleans is a transient community—only a few regulars can endure the smothering wet heat of the long summer—but anyone who passes through leaves traces on other lives and will be remembered months and even years later.

To some extent this special closeness is a result of geography. Street performing in New Orleans is strictly limited to three places in the French Quarter: Jackson Square, and Bourbon and Royal streets, which are cordoned off from vehicle traffic during certain times of the day. The Square is the center, with its park and wide surrounding mall and cafés. Along the north side Chartres Street becomes a broad cobbled space on which front three ancient stone buildings: the Cabildo, St. Louis Cathedral, and the Presbytere. Their long, low porches and stairs make excellent stages and acoustical backdrops for entertainment, while rows of benches provide sitting space for spectators. In the morning performers gather casually here to sit in the sun, share the latest gossip, and observe the passing scene in the leisurely fashion of the South, before going across the Square or off down Royal or Bourbon to work for a while. "Who's down at the Square?" is the standard greeting.

But the French Quarter is not all safe and cozy; there can be an edge of danger in these quaint streets, a feeling of postbellum decadence. Bourbon Street at night is a raucous curb-to-curb party with cafés blasting jazz through open doors and strippers glimpsed in dark bars. The milling crowds carry big paper cups of beer or bourbon, and the nocturnal street performer has both the advantages and the dangers of an audience that is more than a little smashed. The revelry can be seductive, and it takes discipline not to get caught up in the seven-day-a-week party in the Quarter.

A characteristic New Orleans hassle are the black children who tap-dance in the streets. Having no music of their own, they will form a parasitic attachment to a musician, often moving in during the act without asking permission. "They'll pass the hat for you," said Ira the Mime, "and hell—they'll even spend the money for you!" Some performers will stop playing when a tap dancer appears; others negotiate with them for a temporary partnership.

The legality of street performing has been in flux recently in New Orleans, and some very interesting legal precedents have been set, which will be discussed in detail later. The closeness of the street-performing community has made it possible to organize, negotiate, and work with volunteer lawyers in a way that has resulted in some significant actions, but not without a price of days in jail or court for performers.

New Orleans means Mardi Gras to the rest of the world. Dozens and dozens of street acts pour into town for the week-long celebration; performers are on every corner down Bourbon and Royal and every few feet in the Square. Magicians and mimes and jugglers share new tricks and old gossip of their crafts, and musicians jam far into the night. Those who have come expecting big money, however, are disappointed. The competition is too fierce, the parades and parties and balls too distracting for the tourists. Many of the local people pull back and leave the field for the visitors. "The last few days before Mardi Gras we usually just let it pass," said Scotty Hill, a native of New Orleans and the leader of the Original French Market Jazz Band.

Scotty comes from a family of riverboat pilots, and there was some dismay from his relatives when he chose not to follow the family tradition; but now they have been reconciled to his choice. His broad, pale face with its short blond beard was earnest as he talked about the meaning of Mardi Gras, and there was just a touch of the odd Brooklynesque New Orleans accent in his speech. Mardi Gras "is a happy day, almost a spiritual day," he explained. "For the amount of people partying, it's incredibly peaceful." He described the scene: "We all costume; we meet at my house in the morning. We have a regular old-time brass band get-together and all the friends with their costumes and tambourines and shakers and we just hit it out to the streets. We march; we have a Grand Marshal and we have a beautiful banner. . . . Of course, we wouldn't accept one penny on that day. We make stops and go up somewhere and have a few beers, a little bite to eat at different friends' places, blow the whistle and everybody takes off again. On last Mardi Gras day I looked over my shoulder when we hit Royal Street and you could see umbrellas, sparkling things, and costumes of people as far as the eye could see." The total bacchanal of Fat Tuesday is not always so innocent and idyllic, but it is an experience like nothing else.

Jazz Festival, in April, is another good time for street performers—even better, according to Butch Mudbone, blues guitarist. There are the same big crowds of people, he says, but "they're more interested in coming down for music and food than they are for getting drunk and getting crazy in the streets." Many of the local buskers are hired for Jazz Fes, and there is plenty of opportunity on the streets for visiting talent.

The New Orleans street style is funky and intense. In contrast to Boston's shiny professionalism, New York's dingy sophistication, and San Francisco's slick gro-

"Who's down at the Square?"
Ira the Mime and Will the Juggler trade gossip

tesquerie, the New Orleans busker can look as if he slept in a doorway, but he's got to play superbly. In the city of music, where great jazz blows from every café, musical mediocrity is lost in the shuffle. Visual acts have less fierce competition, but they must be flexible enough to deal with anything in this edge-of-danger city.

———————————————•———————————————

IRA BUYS LUNCH

It was getting on toward two o'clock, and I was hungry and heading for lunch. In the Square I met Ira. "Hey, I'm going to Buster Holmes's for red beans and rice—want to come?" I asked.

"Okay, but wait just a minute; I gotta get some money," he said. He went off down Royal Street, and halfway down the block I could see him shift into his hunched-back robot mime walk. In a second a small crowd gathered and hid his tall purple figure from me. I sat down on a bench to wait. It was warm in the sun, and a fly buzzed near my hand. Two little black children ran laughing by, and the cathedral bells rang flatly. In a few moments Ira was back, dumping change out of his rusty top hat. There were several bills and a shower of quarters. "Seven twenty-five, fifty, eight dollars," he counted. "Okay, let's go—I'm buying."

Unlike the big four, where a performer can work the sidewalks every day, most U.S. cities that tolerate busking have only scattered and weekend action. Los Angeles is typical. Although there is an active street-performing scene on weekends nearly all year round, it is very difficult for the full-time busker to make a living there. The only good places are Venice Beach on Saturday and Sunday, and Westwood Village on Friday and Saturday evenings. The serious performer must hit the streets at dusk on Friday evening and work almost continuously (with three changes of location) until sundown Sunday. Faced with almost thirty straight hours of performance, musicians sometimes resort to the artificial energy of amphetamines, and mimes and magicians put in eight or ten hours and then supplement their street income with other jobs.

Los Angeles is not a pedestrian city, and even Venice Beach is on wheels—roller skates and bicycles. This waterfront community has a long tradition of public eccentricity. The Southern California branch of the Beat poets flourished there, and the sad, crazy flower children of the sixties lived and died in hordes on its beach. Nowadays it has become chi-chi for the smart set to roller-skate on the Ocean Front Walk in little satin shorts and to sit drinking Perrier or white wine at its sidewalk cafés, while we colorful local inhabitants continue our lives, observed. On warm Sundays hawkers with carts and wagons and makeshift stalls sell everything from piroshki to hot links, balloon vendors and batik-makers float their wares overhead, and beach dwellers down on their luck spread blankets by the sidewalk and lay out their surplus shirts and paperbacks for sale. Such an atmosphere is fertile ground for street performing, and the Sunday lineup on the walk is impressive (but more fun when the tourists go home). Regulars like Swami X and Jingles share space with itinerants doing a couple of days in L.A. before heading for San Francisco.

Westwood Village, on the edge of the UCLA campus, has a less relaxed ambience. The sidewalks of its planned-crooked streets on Friday and Saturday night are jammed with moviegoers and bored fraternity and high school kids looking for action. The roads are clogged with cars whose owners drive around and around seeking a nonexistent place to park. There is a nervous excitement in the air, and the noise and auto-exhaust pollution levels are high. A musician working Westwood has to be loud, but those performers who can surmount the tumult find Westwood lucrative.

Other spots in Los Angeles sustain a scattering of street performers: Hollywood Boulevard at night ("Scary!" say most buskers), the Music Center plaza before performances, the County Art Museum terrace, or Redondo Beach Pier on Sunday afternoon.

Key West is a useful winter refuge for East Coast buskers. The action there is limited to one small area for two hours a day, but some knowledgeable performers—the Locomotion Vaudeville, Will the Juggler—praise it highly. Just before dusk performers gather at Mallory Square and the pier. "Everybody comes out to celebrate the sunset," says Will. The timing is exact—one hour before sundown and one hour after. The crowd is in a good mood, starting off for an evening of fun. Because of the close quarters, musicians tend to drown each other out, but visual acts do very well. The peak of the season is midwinter, so many performers hibernate here for the cold months.

Occasional buskers are apt to appear almost anywhere, as local talent explores public acceptance or traveling performers run out of cash and are forced to try out new territory. Some itinerants survive nicely on the road by doing hit-and-run performances on college campuses at lunchtime. A very few, who are blessed with more than average charisma and chutzpah, risk misunderstanding and jail on the streets of small towns. Will the Juggler has evolved an on-the-road technique that he finds practical: the first thing he does in a small town is find the sheriff or go to the police station, where he shows them his equipment—

41

torches, swords—and asks permission to perform. "Three out of five times I get an okay," he says.

Festivals and fairs of all kinds are the frosting on the cake for buskers. The Renaissance Faire circuit, especially, is congenial for some kinds of street entertainers. Magicians and mimes and jugglers and rope walkers who can make the necessary historical adaptations in costume and patter are usually welcome, although they are required to audition ahead of time and sometimes must attend workshops in spoken Shakespearean if they are new on the circuit. City festivals like Boston's First Night or Los Angeles' Street Scene hire and/or tolerate free-lance performers. Urban block parties and street fairs abound in summer, as do county and state fairs. Most thoughtful performers agree that fair management should pay them at least a stipend in addition to allowing hat privileges, and more festivals each year are coming to adopt this enlightened position.

Stephen Baird, the diminutive musician who battled for the Boston license, is convinced that college campuses are the natural arena for itinerant buskers. He has fought long and hard to win acceptance for himself and his fellow performers on the lawns of academe. "I'm trying to legalize college campuses nationally, and that's a project that's been six years, and I'm now in the final stages of it. At least there's now ten campuses in the United States where you can just walk in and sing. It's opening up—it's a very lucrative market. If the university can set aside an area for vending machines, they can set aside an area for free speech—both outside and inside." Stephen's sense of responsibility toward the whole phenomenon of street performing has made him a focal point for the network, at least in the eastern part of the United States, and his newsletter, which he mails periodically to several hundred other buskers, is an ongoing analysis of the good places.

MUSICIANS: SOLOISTS

"I got my first guitar when I was fourteen,
Now, I'm over thirty and still wearin' jeans."
—"Amanda" (Country Western song)

The man with the guitar is the basic street performer in America. Unfortunately, singing and playing the acoustic guitar is one of the most difficult ways for a busker to make a living. In an active street scene where every other kind of performer is drawing crowds, the guitarists, because they are so common, will often be ignored by passersby. The instrument is not inherently suitable for the street because its natural voice is quiet, intimate, reflective. To project, many guitarists invest in an amplifier and then try to sing loudly enough to match the artificial sound. The electric guitar, on the other hand, is too loud for any but the most tolerant outdoor environment and is seldom seen on the street. Those solo guitarists who survive do so by dint of great charisma, or great talent, or great persistence. I have seen all three of these saving graces in action, sometimes all in the same performer.

Kenny Lee of Boston is a prime example of persistence. A pleasant but ordinary-looking slight young man in his mid-twenties, he will stand playing folk songs and his own compositions for hours in locations that other performers spurn. He has traveled and played in clubs all over the South, a part of the country other buskers avoid. Kenny is content to make five or ten dollars an hour, even in Quincy Market, and survives because he keeps at it. Last winter he had to take a job with computers to tide him over, but as soon as it got warm again he went back out on the street.

-------------------•-------------------

KENNY LEE UNDERGROUND

The Boston subway station is clean and well-lighted, and the cars come in with a hiss and a well-mannered rattle. A shiny new ceramic mural gives evidence to determined civic efforts to beautify this transient place; Kenny Lee is also part of that beautification. Behind his open guitar case Kenny stands playing away at a folk song, his light voice competing with tunnel noises of comings and goings. His permit is prominently displayed, although both he and I know that he is bootlegging here at the wrong time and the wrong place. The commuters are not amused by his music; they sit waxen-faced on the long benches, staring at nothing, or pace restlessly up and down the platform glancing at their watches or peering down the tracks for the train. Only an occasional person pauses to listen, to exchange a word with Kenny between songs. He plays doggedly on, and when the car pulls in, a few people file past the case and throw in quarters, dimes. In the comparative quiet after the train leaves he bends to scoop up the change, pushing back his pale, unkempt hair. A young man with a briefcase approaches Kenny, his expensive three-piece suit contrasting with the musician's threadbare jeans, and asks to try the guitar. "I used to play some," he says. Kenny, gentle and pleasant, hands it over, and the man fingers a few chords.

The platform fills again. A rollicking intro, and Kenny is playing "The Man Who Never Returned," the old college hootenanny favorite about Charlie, who was trapped with empty pockets on the Boston subway when the fare was raised unexpectedly. People lift their heads, smile a bit. Kenny finishes the song with a flourish, and for the first time gets applause. But the enthusiasm quickly dissipates in the heavy atmosphere of underground waiting, and again he is playing to dead, closed faces, indifferent comings and goings.

But there are also some giant-sized talents on the street. Butch Mudbone is a musician of great skill and heart, a bluesman passionately devoted to the gutsy, structured Delta style. To hear him belting it out on the streets of New Orleans, his big chrome-faced Dobro guitar flashing, is to begin to understand the meaning of the blues. Butch is a master of street technique—he mugs, he crouches, he snarls, he uses his big voice full out—but never at the cost of distorting the music. "Now I make a living on the street," he says. "Sometimes I make a *good* living on the street." But Butch has served his apprenticeship, paid his dues. When I visited him in New Orleans, he told me a saga of his past on the road and the street full of cold and danger and just barely hanging on.

Born in Pennsylvania, he very early became a wanderer, getting into trouble and then moving on. He spent some time with his Seneca Indian father in Arizona, where he had a go at studying electronic engineering and commercial art in college. But trouble soon forced him to hit the road again with a makeshift band. During a stint in the army his musical ability began to gain him notice. He won some talent contests and got an offer from a manager that brought him to Venice Beach and left him in the midst of the hippies of the late sixties, where "a whole bunch of weird things were happening." Butch's life fell apart and he got into heavy drugs. "Oh, I skunked through a trip!"

Butch was salvaged by Uncle Bill Crawford, a great middle-aged bluesman from North Carolina, whose park-bench wisdom and magnificent Delta blues guitar have been a fixture in Venice as long as anybody can remember. Uncle Bill's protégés include some famous jazz names, including—it is rumored—Janis Joplin. Butch says, "Uncle Bill told me, 'Look, all you need is that guitar. You know how to play blues—anybody can play blues.' And he got me all into it, and he got me so involved in it, and I can never thank him enough."

Beginning to play on the street a little, Butch joined forces with a one-handed Venice musician named Hook. They formed a group called The Canaligators and were soon off on the road again, playing impromptu gigs in seedy bars and on the streets, traveling through Chicago's winter cold and down the East Coast. They shivered in their California clothes, ate when they could afford it, smiled at pretty girls in hopes of a warm place to spend the night. "But when you're on the road, and you don't have any rent to pay, who cares. If you've got enough

Butch Mudbone belts out the blues

money to keep yourself in strings and picks and clothes and food—what else?

"I slept with my arms around the guitar always on the road. It was understood that you don't let your guitar out of your sight and preferably not out of your hands. Because if some guy comes up on the street and says 'I play guitar, let me play your guitar a second,' you don't let him play, because then everybody else wants to do it too. Either that or he says, 'Well, thanks for the guitar, chump,' and that's that. We had to fight a few times, over things like that, or money. . . . Street life is . . . I don't know how many times I've come close to getting shot or cut or something like that. I've been through a lot of those deals. I got beat up down here one night by a bunch of bikers. I give 'em my licks, but I wasn't big enough to fight their badass fightin'." Butch shook his head reminiscently. "Me and Hook had a lot of times like that—we both had our backs to the wall."

Butch is young, but he has lived hard, the kind of life that qualifies him to sing the blues, for the blues are of the earth and the body, a music that teaches the acceptance of life, reflected in the strong, solid structure, the heavy inevitability of the beat, the sureness of the repeated phrases.

He picked up the guitar and explained some of the harmonic shape of the Delta style, playing the changes with intricacy and consummate skill. "I appreciate more of a tight form of expression," he said. "Muddy Waters, now. All of his stuff on the albums was real precise, like 'Rock Me, Baby.' He did four times, each time. After four times on the lick that he does after the verse, he goes to the eight, he does the verse, then he comes back and he does it four times, and it's right on the numbers, every time. And I appreciate that, it's beautiful. But it's simple. It's very hard to be that simple."

He invoked some of the great names of the barrelhouse circuit—Leadbelly, Blind Lemon Jefferson, Blind Blake— who played "anyplace they could get their foot in the door —barbecues, house-rent parties, bars, and clubs—if they couldn't get their foot in the door, then they did it outside." The traveling bands, too, like Muddy Waters, Howlin' Wolf, would play where they could. "If they couldn't find a place to play, then they'd just play out on the street." Scotty Hill and jazz historian Bill Russell had told me of the days when New Orleans merchants would hire bands to play in mule-drawn wagons advertising clothing stores or boxing matches; they told tales of jazz funeral processions, black children's "spasm bands" with homemade instruments . . . and as Butch talked I had a vision of a jazz street tradition and this young former Californian as a legitimate carrier of that tradition.

Butch's devotion to the blues led him inevitably to New Orleans, first to a Mardi Gras in 1968, and then for visits from Venice more and more often, until several years ago he came to stay. He and his wife are respected members now of the French Quarter community. He has a band for indoor gigs, and he plays often at clubs and parties as well as the street. He was one of the stars at Jazz Festival last year. But sometimes he chafes at the impermanence and lack of recognition on the street. "I want to do some recording—I don't want to do stuff on the street the rest of my life. At least I can have an album that I can send to my mother and my sister and some of the people I ain't seen in ten or twelve years. 'Cause they don't know, all they know is I'm playing on the street and they don't think much of it. It's not getting famous, or getting popular, it's just getting well known enough that you can make a living in the clubs and have the gigs and have the recording abilities and chances. See, once I get my name on a record and I'm known as being a *good* musician, somebody people can listen to over the years—I feel that's necessary."

A few performers survive on charisma. That elusive something that has been called "star quality," in the overworked Hollywood phrase, is immediately apparent in the close performer-audience relationship of the street. It is rare, but it is unmistakable. And the strange thing is that it is only marginally related to ability. These are the people who draw crowds before they open their mouths, and who are deluged with money and gifts and love when they finish their acts, whether they're any good or not. The point is that they leave their audience feeling that they have been dusted with enchantment.

With some of them, this magnetic quality carries over into their personal lives, and Peter Damien is one of these. To sit on a bench on the beach with Peter is like watching some kindly feudal lord holding court. Passersby greet him, stop to talk, give him things, other musicians come by to jam—a constant stream of tribute. He is humbly aware of his own magic; I asked him when he first became aware of it. "When I noticed that I got everything I wanted," he said. "I've been granted it by the Good Lord."

Most street musicians dream of the day they will make it big. Peter is unique in that he has already made it big and gave it up for the simpler life of the street. Born a Canadian in extreme poverty, he became a nightclub star in Detroit, where his raspy voice and pounding guitar earned him the title of "The Joe Cocker of Canada." He came to California "chasing my dreams," left his manager, and is now living happily in his car on the beach. "The money makes us crazy," he said. "I chased it in Detroit, and I had it all to give it up. And now I have it greater. Here in Venice I'm treated with elegance."

———————————————•———————————————

PETER DAMIEN LANDS IN THE SLAMMER

Here they come down Bourbon Street, small dark-bearded Phoenix with his saxophone case and big, hearty Peter, spreading his wide leather cape to give me a hug. "Hey, good to see home folks from Venice! Where you guys been?" I ask. "I haven't seen you around for days. I thought the Mardi Gras swallowed you. Are you okay?"

"We are now," says Phoenix grimly. "Peter's been in jail. He just got out."

"Yeah, I was in for two and a half days. It was heavy—really heavy." Peter shakes his head.

"My God, what for?" I ask. I had heard that New Orleans street performers were being arrested last month, but this was Mardi Gras, and the heat was off. "What did you do?"

"I was just sitting quietly on the levee with some people, smoking a joint, when this guy next to me asks for a hit. When I pass it to him, he flashes his badge and tells me I'm under arrest for possession."

"Are you kidding? In this drug city they busted you for one toke?"

"Yeah, they busted everybody. They handcuffed me to this other guy and they shoved us all in the Black Maria, and took us down to the jail and put us in the tank." Peter's broad, handsome face is pale from his ordeal, but freshly shaven. "We're going to get something to eat now; come on along."

Over red beans and rice Peter can't stop talking about it. His husky voice is intense. "They stripped us naked, and made us walk single file down a corridor with our hands over our heads, and they searched us everywhere. Then they gave us prison clothes to wear and they sprayed us with bug-killer—that's part of the humiliation. In the tank there were all these very heavy dudes, and when somebody new came in they'd shove them up against the wall and feel their muscles to see if they could get away with anything. The guards kept saying stuff to get you mad so they could beat up on you, but I stayed cool. There were these foam rubber mattresses on the floor but not enough of them, and when some guy wanted mine I just backed off: 'Hey, that's cool, take it man. I'll sleep on the floor.' I wasn't going to get my head kicked in. There was only one toilet and you had to shit right in front of everybody. And the food was

Phoenix and Peter

awful stuff; I couldn't eat it!" He forks up beans and sausage appreciatively. Across the table Phoenix has taken out his little soprano sax and is improvising softly with the jukebox.

Peter finishes his plate and lights a cigarette reflectively. "But you know, people really shared, too. They passed around their cigarettes, and we talked—there's nothing to do but talk. For two days I heard everything about other guys' lives. Some of those black dudes have had bad times." His eyes are wide with the remembered despair of the lives he has just recently touched. "Some of them weren't going to get bailed out; they had nobody to call or their relatives were tired of getting them out. They were going to be there for months. When I left I took a bunch of messages and phone numbers to call . . ."

There is a nudge on the back of my chair, and a woman says, "Could you move a little please so I can get through?" Peter's charm bursts out like the sun coming from behind a cloud. "I tell you what, we'll move if you'll give me a kiss," he beams. She giggles, and then agrees. I shift the chair and she bends over Peter. He gives her a good one, and she goes away laughing.

"How did you get bailed out?" I ask.

"Well, that's what took so long," Phoenix explains. "When we first got separated and it got to be midnight, I said to myself, 'Peter's either found a fine lady or he's in jail.' By the next morning I was saying, 'That certainly must have been a fine lady!' and by noon I knew he was in jail somewhere."

"But I couldn't phone him," Peter takes up the story, "because we've been sleeping in the car. So the Mardi Gras Coalition—they're these young lawyers that volunteer to help out-of-town people that get into trouble—found him for me. I gave them his description, and after two days their aides spotted him on the street."

"Even then we weren't out of the woods," continued Phoenix. "After I paid the bail I was waiting for Peter behind the jail building, and he came out the front door and missed me. He was walking around all night looking for me."

Peter finishes his coffee and pushes back his chair, restored and ready for action. "Well, we're all right now, and from here on we're going to enjoy the Mardi Gras."

"Great. I noticed a sign on the door about a private party in this café tonight—I'll go see if we can play for them," says Phoenix the manager. In a minute he is back. "Okay, they say we can do it. Let's go wash up at Butch's and then play for a while on the street."

"All right!" says Peter, lifting his guitar case. "Let's go make some music!"

Next to the guitar the banjo is probably the most common American street instrument, although it is most often seen in duo with the guitar or as a component of bluegrass or Dixieland bands, and less often as a solo pitch. The banjo is reputed to be difficult, and many musicians progress to it after mastering the guitar.

Stu Buck started with the guitar, and then switched to the autoharp, which he chose after being inspired by Mike Seeger, and because there are "not a lot of autoharp players around. No matter how I play it, there's not a big group to judge it by." For those who associate the autoharp with the laps of kindergarten teachers, Stu's playing is a surprise. He holds it snuggled up against his shoulder and tucked under his ear in the new style invented when the instrument was redesigned in the early sixties. He uses a small amplifier to project its delicate sound, and he sings and dances to his own music. His repertoire is mostly Country Western, bluegrass, ragtime standards.

Stu has come to the street by a circuitous route. Now in his early thirties, he has a bachelor's degree in psychology and is just a few units short of a master's in criminal justice. He was heading toward being the director of a mental health program and had gotten as far as a job as a drug counselor, when "it suddenly dawned on me that this was not what I wanted to do." For a while he lost his direction and worked at a variety of things ranging from research assistant to construction worker to probation officer. At last he realized that music was his love, but before making a full-time commitment to it he wanted to be in charge of his life. This he accomplished by working as an account executive at radio stations WKTK and WBMD in Baltimore, where he learned the music business and had his own program. In 1978, deciding that the time was right, he came to New Orleans "just to see if I could play on the street and make a few cents." He could, and he has been there ever since, although he occasionally has to do substitute teaching to eke out the rent on his garret apartment in the Quarter. "When I'm playing out on the street and people watch and go by and smile and have a good time, I feel I'm making more of a contribution to humanity, to mental health, than I did when I was in a classic, so-called helping profession." Stu Buck was born Stuart Buchwald and comes from a middle-class Jewish background in Baltimore. "What does your family feel about your playing on the street?" I asked him. "They think I'm crazy," he said.

The guitar is also an instrument for classical music, and in the second chapter we met Don Gribble, a former teacher, who plays Bach and Villa-Lobos at the cable car turnaround in San Francisco—wearing a rusty tailcoat and top hat, in keeping with that city's taste for the colorful. The violin, too, has a double personality: classical and traditional American. In the second identity it is called the fiddle and is an important part of bluegrass, Cajun, and old-time American music. The fiddle is almost never seen on the street alone—fiddlers being in high demand as members of bands—although one of the first street performers to catch my imagination was the legendary Henry the Fiddler, who sometimes passed through Venice possessing only his fiddle, his backpack, and his own soul. The classical violinist, on the other hand, is not too unusual as a street solo. One of the most memorable is New York's Gudrun Schaumann, whose beauty and long red hair are as startling as the clarity of her bowing.

When considering classical music on the streets, it is well to remember that, as Ghirardelli's Marsha Monro put it, "People in the classical groups are generally graduate students in music and basically are just rehearsing." A classical violinist who is a true street performer—the original street performer, if we accept his own evaluation—is Richard Wexler, the Carnegie Hall Violinist. Richard works intermissions and exits on Broadway's Shubert Alley, and his partner in the act is a dog, a matronly spaniel named Come Here. She, in her territorial doggie way, considers Broadway her turf, and will bark indignantly at other dog trespassers, or at policemen's horses. Come Here enjoys performing, although her part of the show is just to sit politely on a little rug in front of the violin case while Richard plays. She likes to be in place before the crowd comes out of the theater—if they arrive late, she sulks and is annoyed with Richard. The two of them ride in cabs from one theater foyer to the next with split-second timing. ("This is my slow night," Richard told me on a Monday when he was doing four intermissions and three exits.) Richard is a star. He is also an excellent violinist, but that has very little to do with it. He has an extraordinary power of evocation: "I am totally a fantasy object," he says. "They can make anything they want out of me."

A good street-performing act is like a pilot light, he explained to me. People come to it, and sometime back in their past they have put aside the idea that they might be a dancer or an artist or a musician. Everybody has had some such dream, but they've put it aside and gone on with their humdrum life. And then they see the street performer and see that "somebody is managing to get away with it, with life, and managing to live between the cracks. 'I may never do it,' they say, 'but if *somebody's* doing it, it means my dream is still alive, and that maybe one day I'll do it—it's not too late.' And that's what a street performer is."

Richard is indeed one of the original modern street performers in this country. He began fifteen years ago, and sees himself as a catalyst for all that followed. "I was proof that you could do it and survive—that nobody would kill you. And that you could even get praised for it." His publicity has helped to legitimize street performing; he has been on the Johnny Carson show and the Merv Griffin show, and has been written about in major newspapers and magazines all over the world.

He traced his own beginnings: "As children we are all street performers. When our parents used to yell at us 'Go out and play!' we all did. We went out and played and we had a good time. And I always tell people that the difference between me and most people is that I continued playing and everybody else went inside and settled down.

"I've always expected to get rewarded for performing. I was an excellent show-and-tell person in school. It's never seemed strange to me to get paid on the street. That's one reason I've succeeded as a street performer—because I expected people to give me money—I couldn't understand it if they didn't. I was *amazed* if someone could not give me money."

And give him money they do. Richard came to our appointment on a snow-white Moped, dressed in an elegant silk shirt of European cut open to the navel, with a heavy gold necklace and a huge digital watch. But on his feet were the same broken shoes from his performance the night before ("I have terrible feet," he explained). "I've always made sure that people realize that I make a lot of money, because that's what they want to realize. They want me to go home in a limousine. That's why I always take cabs. When somebody says, 'Oh, you take cabs!' I say, 'Just because my chauffeur's sick.'

"They say to me, 'You must make a fortune!' and I answer, 'Well, how much do you think I make?'

"They'll say, 'I bet you make five hundred dollars a week.'

"I say, 'Five hundred a week? You think I'd stand here and do this for five hundred? I could make that selling vacuum cleaners. You call five hundred a week a lot of money? Boy, what do you make? I make so much more than five hundred a week . . . I tell you, I make triple that!'

"They say, 'Are you crazy? You don't make fifteen hundred dollars out there!'

"I say, 'You think not, huh? I tell you what, tomorrow afternoon you come along with me to my financial advisor's office and we'll look at my stock portfolio . . .' and they really believe it."

———————————————————●———————————————————

ENCOUNTER AT INTERMISSION

"I'll be at *The Elephant Man* intermission at 9:03 if you want to see me performing," he had said on the phone. But the taxi is slow, the traffic heavy, and when the driver lets me out in front of the theater, a crowd of well-dressed people is already standing about, smoking and chatting. I hear the high, thin tones of a violin, and I see a knot of people gathered near the entrance. I edge through the crowd and look over their shoulders. A man is playing, his face rapt, lost in the music. Mendelssohn is it? Or Schumann? Before him is an open case and a dog, a plump apricot spaniel sitting on a little blue rug. Who is this person, this excellent musician, what has brought him to such humble straits? His face is sensitive, pointed, and intense, with fierce but kind eyes and a shock of collar-length dark hair. His jeans are ancient but clean and neatly patched. He wears a shabby sweater, but it is a perfect fit over his slimly elegant torso. A romantic scarf is knotted at his throat. And the shoes—ah, the heartbreaking shoes! Cracked, split, showing his socks—but immaculately polished. Maudlin fantasies of Parisian garrets float through my head, starving music students, poor but proud . . . The dog brings me back to reality; with the same pointed face and gentle eyes as her master's, she is faintly comic as she sits gazing about at the people, waving the tip of her tail tentatively with restrained anxiety to please. The lobby lights blink, and the people begin to put out cigarettes and drift back into the theater. Most of them drop money into the case as they enter, and a few stop to speak to the violinist for a moment. I stand back, suddenly shy. When the last elegant lady has left, I bend to stroke the dog's silky ears. "Her hair is the same color as yours," says Richard Wexler.

The accordion would seem to be the perfect street instrument: portable, versatile, loud, easy to play, a whole orchestra in a box. But for those very reasons it is tainted by its association with the era of maimed beggars and is not as common as would be supposed. There are still a few elderly men who squeeze out tunes on the street—J. W. Riggs of Boston, for one, who lives in a nursing home but uses his music as an excuse to get out and meet people.

Patrick White of Venice is the only young accordionist I saw in my travels. Patrick is in his early twenties but seems younger in his innocence. He came to Hollywood from Kansas City to make it as a songwriter. He had learned to play the accordion from his mother, who bought the instrument from a fly-by-night salesman and then taught herself from a book, staying one chapter ahead of her son. Later he went to college on a music scholarship. Patrick belongs to the musician's union and is doing quite well at supper clubs with his standard accordion-book repertoire.

The street is transitory for him, and he is not aggressive about hustling money. "The reason I play out in the streets is I love Venice," he smiles mistily. "I'm really a romantic; you should see my room." He glances at his rosy-cheeked girl friend, and she blushes.

The concertina is another ideal street instrument. It is small and compact, the sound carries well, and it stands up to the weather—all reasons why it often was taken to sea by sailors, says David Wyman. David's street image is seagoing: a leather visored cap, a blue scarf knotted around his neck, a striped shirt, and an old pea jacket. He sits on an overturned box on the streets of New Orleans and cheerfully plays away at sea chanties, polkas, children's songs like "Pop Goes the Weasel," "Blow the Man Down."

The street is a breathing space for David; he is an actor-puppeteer and has been touring schools and shopping malls in the South on a government program. "I get new energy from the street," he explains. "I've been planning things for four years, and that's enough time. Now I need to get kind of loose and breathe in a little art for a change. Mostly what I want to do while I'm here is use it for a kind of a working playing ground, tighten up my skills and learn some new things." When he is ready to move on he will head for San Francisco, New York, or Europe—the choice is wide.

The piano, of course, is the basic solo instrument in Western culture. The problem with the piano on the street is how to get it there. I have seen the dilemma solved (but only by those who live on the first floor) by mounting it on casters or by encouraging several muscular friends to hang around until quitting time. But the best solution is John Timothy's gimmick in San Francisco. Six years ago, when he was twenty-nine, he found himself down and out with no marketable skills. In a flash of inspiration he borrowed his parents' piano, loaded it on his battered pickup truck, and went downtown to play at the curb. The first day he made thirty dollars, and he has been at it ever since.

He is a landmark at Fisherman's Wharf, where he arrives every morning about nine to get a parking place outside the Cannery. He spends the morning reading the papers and drinking cappucino with friends. About noon, when the tourists are thick, he begins his working day, playing ragtime and a little jazz from his dusty red truck. He is picturesque in his white tie and swallowtail coat, his long blond hair drawn back at the nape under a top hat. Between numbers he pauses to sip wine from a crystal goblet, or passes out long-stemmed red roses to pretty ladies. Timothy is so picturesque, in fact, that this year he has had to post a sign for miserly camera buffs: "It is a San Francisco custom for photographers to tip the performer." I asked, "Is it a good life?" He paused a moment before he answered. "It is in many ways. I'm working for myself and that's always a good feeling. It doesn't mean I'm working any less—in many ways I'm working even more, but I like that kind of independence and freedom."

A magazine article about John Timothy inspired John Bushell to put *his* piano on wheels. Johnny B (his street name) was on the opposite side of the country at the time, playing at Boston's Durgin Park Restaurant. A former elementary school teacher, he was looking for a way to finance some extensive traveling, and when he read about Timothy's musical truck, lights flashed in his head. He rigged up a truly impressive vehicle, a live-in van with a stage for the piano that appeared when the rear doors were let down. He set out to cross the country in September 1979 and found he had no trouble at all making friends and expenses. Johnny B is a sociable soul, and when he pounds out "Beat Me, Daddy, Eight to the Bar" or "Rock Around the Clock," he has a sing-along crowd in no time. Other musicians gather at the foot of his plywood stage to jam with him, and offers of gigs and meals come thick and fast. Johnny B has had none of the usual street performer's hassles with police; he seems to find easy acceptance even when he plays in locations where no other busker would be tolerated—downtown Los Angeles, for instance, or in front of the San Francisco Stock Exchange. Partly this is because his short tubby body and round, happy face exude wholesomeness, but mostly (I suspect) it stems from an American conviction that a man who owns a big vehicle is a man to be respected.

The saxophone is the most commonly seen wind instrument on the street. Phoenix (who got his name when he rose from his own ashes after a serious emotional and physical illness) and Barcelona Red (whose street name comes from his flaming hair and beard) both do well with it. Although the sax is visually and acoustically well-suited for street playing, it is not inherently a solo instrument, and some sax players seem to reach to fill that lack almost unconsciously. Mike Conley tap-dances while he plays, and Cedric Stokes stands on a bass guitar and steps out an accompaniment in his stocking feet.

The flute and the clarinet are also popular wind street instruments. In fact, it is possible to hear almost any of the standard orchestral instruments on the street, either in combinations or as solos. The only ones that I cannot remember seeing are the piccolo and the timpani, although I'm sure it is entirely possible that next week I will turn a corner and there will stand a timpanist passing the hat. However, the best way to make a living from street music is to play something unusual, preferably something that is fun to watch as well as hear, or something that makes people stop in their tracks and ask, "What *is* it?"

The answer to that question, in Scott Alexander's case, is "The Arkansas Beartrap!" This contraption (no other word suits) consists of a chrome-plated washboard mounted on a small table on which are four wooden temple blocks, two cowbells, a tin can with some noisemakers in it, a pair of cymbals—and sometimes a cheese grater. From this pile of junk Scott (who calls himself Professor Washboard) coaxes an astonishing barrage of percussive sound —precise, complex, and almost faster than the ear can follow. He uses a battery-powered amplifier and wears eight copper thimbles on his fingers to increase the sound.

Scott grew up in Arkansas and graduated from college with a degree in rhetoric, but now he lets his fingers do the talking. He has been on the road for a long time, first in Washington, D.C., where he sat in with Irish musicians, and then to Austin, Texas, for a year, and on to the Mardi Gras and a stay in New Orleans. There he teamed up with honky-tonk guitarist Lance Wakeley. The two of them decided it was time to leave town when they were arrested for playing on Royal Street. After a summer stint in Venice, they headed for Europe, and when last heard from they were reputed to be a sensation on the Continent. A tall, rangy redhead with a cleft chin and dimples, Scott has an eye for the ladies, and, like most street performers, he finds the ladies have an eye for him. "When I'm playing, I'm on the make," he told me candidly.

Lance and Scott are on the make in other ways, too. They push hard for money on the street, doing a pickup after every two numbers ("My name's Lance Wakeley, and this here's Professor Washboard. We make our living doing this. . . ."). For a while they used a battery-powered robot to pass their hat; few people were able to ignore its outthrust hand, especially when the mechanical collector had the rapt attention of everyone else in the audience. The police soon decided to define that ploy as soliciting, so they went back to the hard verbal sell. There is always a fine line between accepting money for entertainment and soliciting it, and street performers are keenly aware of the difference. The open guitar case or the hat set out for contributions, even with a sign or a verbal pitch asking for money, are very different in the eyes of the law from passing among the crowd with a container for donations. The latter is confused with begging, and will often bring official wrath down on the head of a performer. However, hat-passing is so much more lucrative that many will chance it when they are in need of money.

Lance and Scott give value for payment received, playing at full energy for hours and hours. During their summer in Los Angeles they performed in Westwood Village and at Venice Beach almost continuously from eight o'clock Friday night to five o'clock Sunday evening. The rest of the week they recovered from the grueling weekend marathon, sleeping until noon, following up on phone numbers dropped in their hat, trying out new music, and at night hanging out in clubs to sit in with the musicians or try out in talent contests. One afternoon every week was reserved for rolling the change, a constant chore for successful performers. Banks frown on pounds of loose silver dumped out on the teller's counter, so it is necessary to count out stacks of nickels and dimes and quarters and roll them in brown paper cylinders before exchanging them for bills.

Both Lance and Scott are committed to the street, although they occasionally talk about making an album or taking on an agent. Butch Mudbone told me, "Lance used to have a group called Joyous Noise. I think he intended at the beginning not to be a street musician but to put together a band, doing recording sessions and all that. But now, he's geared for the street. He doesn't even really think about doing anything else but the street." Barcelona Red agreed: "Lance really considers himself a street musician; although he might play some club dates once in a while, he's not too much into it because he can make so much more money on the street with so much less trouble."

Percussionists are not usually loners on the street. They

Scott Alexander, alias Professor Washboard (small picture) and his partner Lance Wakeley look for chances to join other musicians and add a melodic line to their rhythm. Not so with Beppo, a strange little black man from France, who resents insensitive jamming. Beppo is a solo act, in life as well as in performance. He grew up on the outskirts of Paris, and as a baby he was dropped on his head. He blames the accident for a variety of physical ills—a wall-eye, one leg shorter than the other. He worked for a time as a cook, but got into trouble with chefs because he would not follow the rules. "I needed to express my own soul," he explained. His performance on the bongo drums is haunting—compositions using rhythm, explosive tongue-clicks, an eerie saxophone-like voice line. "What is that you're singing?" I asked after listening closely several times. "Is it French?"

"It is no national language," he confided hesitantly. "It is the language of my soul."

A more conventional drummer is Don Hill, whose home base is in Detroit. Don, a tall, handsome, bearded black man, uses his natural leadership abilities to organize drummers' workshops in every city he visits, teaching "ways to be cool and avoid problems and hassles in outdoor drumming." The role of drum suppression in black history is very close to Don's heart, and he discourses well on that subject. Although he can fit in to almost any style of musical group (in New Orleans he even accompanied Will the Juggler), he also can do African solos on his big conga drums, singing in languages as exotic as Bambara.

It is true that drums have a decibel problem on the street, because the sound of that instrument was originally designed to carry for long distances. The same is true of the bagpipes, which need to be heard on a Highland cliff to be really appreciated. Bagpipes are unbearable indoors to many non-Scots, so pipers will often be found on the street because they need a place to practice. I had thought the pipes took enormous lung power and strength until I

Beppo in New Orleans

encountered a frail-looking lass playing outside St. Thomas Church on Fifth Avenue. She had just recently come to New York to study Highland dancing, and her sound was as full-bodied as that of any male who ever wore the sporran.

The steel drums can also be piercing and penetrating, with a sound that carries excitement for blocks. The world's greatest solo virtuoso on the steel drums is undoubtedly Victor Brady, who calls himself "the grandfather of all street musicians." He has been a busker for thirteen years, and to hear him performing the adagio from the "Moonlight Sonata," or the "Minute Waltz," under the arch in Washington Square is one of the most memorable street experiences. He prefers to call the instrument the "steel piano" ("*Steel drum* is what it's made from," he says), a name that does come closer to conveying its sweet, bell-like tone. His repertoire is largely classical, although he does not read music. "I want to show the world that I can take a simple garbage can and play music that was created by geniuses on other instruments," he explains.

Victor started on the street almost accidentally; during the mayoral election of 1967 he played at campaign stops to draw a crowd for John Lindsay; people began to ask him, "Why don't you pass the hat?" Since then he has gained worldwide recognition—a tour of Europe playing night clubs and concerts, a command performance before the Queen of Denmark, several record albums, television appearances with Johnny Carson and Merv Griffin, and a recent Las Vegas show where he shared billing with Charo and Jack Jones. Victor Brady may hold the American record for largest contribution ever received on the street. A German gentleman watched him play the "Minute Waltz" and was moved to empty his pockets of $158.03.

The hammer dulcimer (not to be confused with the mountain dulcimer) is an excellent street instrument; its sound is appealing, it has a distinctive literature of suitable music, it is fascinating to watch, and it is unusual enough to arouse curiosity. Hammer dulcimer players fall in love with the instrument and become passionately involved with its construction and history, and many of them play instruments that they have made themselves. Kansas City dulcimer player Matt Kirby shared his extensive knowledge of its lore with me: Similar instruments exist in other cultures—the santur of Iran, the cimbalom of Hungary. The American version was patented in the 1860s, and for a time was enormously popular—end tables that open out into dulcimers appear in the Montgomery Ward catalog as late as 1910. Its place in American living rooms was taken over by the piano around the turn of the century, and it fell into neglect. Before its revival in New England in

1968, only two or three people in the United States remembered how to play it. Today there are enough cultists to support a newsletter called *The Dulcimer Players News*, and a national championship at the Winfield Folk Festival.

Similar in appearance to a large zither, the dulcimer is played with two padded mallets, either on a stand or flat on the sidewalk with the musician on his knees. Matt describes it as a combination of percussion and melody— "every drumbeat is its own note." The challenge is that only two tones can be sounded at once, although the hammers can be quickly rolled to approximate chords. It is fun to watch; Matt says, "There's a sense of mystery about the instrument because so much sound comes out of it and yet the hammers move so quickly and you don't see it."

In my conversations with hammer dulcimerists I found that they tended to know each other, at least by reputation. I spoke with five members of the fraternity. Matt Kirby has played in Boston and Kansas City and will head for Boulder soon. His repertoire is mainly Scottish (although he played "Jesu, Joy of Man's Desiring" for me), and he has recently evolved a street image as the Liberace of the Dulcimer, wearing a tuxedo and illuminating his performance with a candelabrum. Doug Berch was part of the Color by Number String Band the day I heard him in New York's Financial District. He travels the bluegrass and old-time music festival circuit, and when last seen was heading toward Philadelphia to work with a musical-instrument maker. Rain or Shine is a San Francisco pair of dulcimerists, Mark Davis and John Lionarons, who take turns on their one instrument. They met at college in Buffalo, and their lives converged when they met again on the street in Boulder. Mark has taught industrial arts, and John is heading for a career as an actor. Their repertoire is Irish and traditional American, and Mark has added a few Greek pieces that were originally composed for the bouzouki. Dorothy Carter of Cambridge is something of the high priestess of street dulcimerists, although she was amused when I mentioned her reputation, and disclaimed it. "I actually played on the street only one summer three or four years ago," she laughed. But six months later I turned a corner in New Orleans and found Dorothy and her beautiful teen-age daughter, Celeste, spread out on the sidewalk making music for an entranced circle of squatting admirers. They were on a gypsy tour, she explained as wisps of her long reddish hair blew about her elfin face, and were traveling the country, staying with friends in one town and another. The police had just impounded her car for illegal parking, and they were raising its ransom on the street, playing and selling her record albums. Dorothy's music has an unearthly, mystical quality, and goes far beyond the forthright dance tunes that are usually played on the hammer dulcimer. She was one of the rediscoverers of the instrument and is respected in musicology

The hammer dulcimer (Mark Davis's hands)

circles. She often gives lecture-concerts of international traditional music for esoteric instruments at colleges and summer festivals.

The one-man band is a true street phenomenon, and its fascination lies not in the quality of the music but in the inventiveness of the arrangement. Just to watch one mouth, one pair of hands and feet, manipulating a wild assemblage of noisemakers is wonder enough. One would think that the American genius for inventiveness would be particularly at home with the one-man band, but although I heard tales of San Francisco's Hokum Jeebs and Professor Gizmo, the only such musician I actually saw other than Professor Washboard was a foreigner—Frank Runaud of Canada. His knitted cap pulled down over his ears would have hinted at his nationality for me, even if I had not seen the red and white maple-leaf flag that topped his creation. His autonomous orchestra has evolved over the last two and half years. He began with a small accordion and a tambourine that he played with his foot. Gradually other elements were added, until now his instrument consists of a washboard mounted upright, a pair of foot pedals that work a drum and a flat cymbal and that jar an upright tambourine on a little table on which stands a clown doll that can be swiveled to play a toy xylophone, above which is a curled hose ending in a trumpet bell topped by a faded parasol. On a separate stand are a set of bongos with bulb horns attached, and Frank wears a harmonica rack with whistles and tooters and shakes a wooden eagle-headed Indian rattle while he plays the accordion. The surprisingly pleasant and amusing music that emerges from all of this conglomeration are Eastern European waltzes and polkas, since Frank originally came from that part of the world.

As pleasant and amusing as his music, he told me his romantic history. When he was a child, his father was conscripted into the Russian army, and Frank and his mother, as Jews, were deported to the north. There she got a job on a circus train caring for the animals at night. They traveled across Russia to Central Asia and lived across the border from Afghanistan. From there he came eventually to California, and then during the Korean War to Canada, where he settled down in British Columbia. He and his exquisite French Canadian wife have a small farm where they live with their two beautiful little daughters. During the tourist season in Vancouver, Frank plays on the streets for extra money to get them through the year. They had come to the Mardi Gras (where I saw them) following a lifelong dream to spend some time in the bayou absorbing Cajun music. "We had to kill all the chickens so we could come," he said, smiling.

Certainly the most unusual street music in America is played by Jim Prichard Turner in Philadelphia. Jim is a serious performer and lecturer on the musical glasses, and has appeared as a soloist with the Denver Symphony and as a three-time guest on the Johnny Carson show. The history of the musical glasses is closely linked with that of an ill-fated instrument invented by Benjamin Franklin called the glass harmonica. Both work on the principle of utilizing the tone produced when a moistened fingertip is rotated on the edge of a glass container. The glass harmonica, however, was an arrangement of meshing glass bowls strung on a spindle that was rotated by a foot pedal. It leaped into popularity almost immediately after its invention by Franklin, and works were composed for it by Mozart, Handel, Beethoven, and a number of lesser musicians. Glass-harmonica concerts were all the rage for several years, until it began to be noticed that every virtuoso on the instrument lost his mind shortly after rising to fame. Some still unknown quality of its vibration produced irreversible nerve damage. It was reluctantly abandoned, and the music that had been written for it was forgotten.

Until Jim Prichard Turner. He is not foolish enough to attempt to revive the glass harmonica (although Franklin's own instrument has just been given to the Franklin Institute, and Turner gave a cautious concert on it last spring). The instrument he does play was its precursor and consists of thirty-nine water-filled brandy snifters arranged for easy chord reach on a collapsible table at which he sits, dips his finger in distilled water, and produces not only Beethoven, Mozart, and Handel but also "Die Lorelei," "When the Saints Come Marching In," and the "Beer Barrel Polka."

Jim has earned his living with the musical glasses, the clarinet, and the chime-wrench for many years, but he is a newcomer to the street. In the summer of 1979 he began to play on the Boulder Mall in Colorado. When he moved to Philadelphia he finished out the season on the streets of that city. "It was a revelation to me," he said, "that one could make a living that way. Playing on the street is very special. There is a vulnerability, but a contact, too." He draws huge crowds, and has not been immune to street hassles. Playing at Penthouse Square one evening, he was approached by a belligerent drunk, who staggered up and challenged him in the midst of a Beethoven piece with "How ya doin' that?" Turner finished the selection ("You have to be centered on the street"), and, believing in the soothing power of the musical glasses, showed him how to dip his finger in water and produce a tone. The drunk was delighted. He stayed quietly through the rest of the concert and then floundered back to his car to get some money to put in the hat.

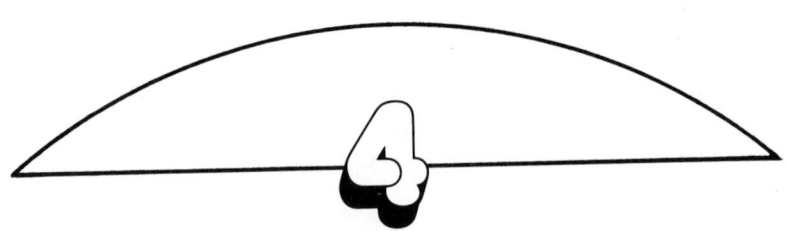

MUSICIANS:
DUOS AND GROUPS

"I used to need work to fill every hour;
I needed to feel that feeling of power."
—"I Don't Need Anything But You," from *Annie*
(lyrics by Martin Charnin)

The musical team of Roselyn Lionhart and David Leonard is of long duration—twenty-one years. "Seems like yesterday," said David. "Seems like forever," said Roselyn. They have four children: two college-age daughters, three-year-old Autumn Rose, and a son born in March 1980 and named David Stormborn in memory of the rainy circumstances of his birth. They are both accomplished musicians and singers, but together they are an interesting complement and contrast. David, with his flowing white hair and genial eyes, is warm and relaxed; Roselyn, with her dark, expressive face and wide mouth, her hair braided in beaded cornrows or tied up in a scarf, is a dormant volcano. Her earthy power is apparent in performance; on the street their delivery is so casual as to seem almost offhand, yet they quickly draw a crowd.

Roselyn's blues singing has been compared to Bessie Smith's. She has a big, gutsy voice when she lets it full out, and David has a sure, pleasant baritone. They harmonize with the empathy of twenty-one years behind them. Their repertoire is folk jazz, a description that includes country blues, Afro rhythms, Arkansas party riddles, Georgia Sea Island chants, spirituals, and their own compositions. Usually David plays the guitar and harmonica, and Roselyn strums the mandolin or her own guitar, but once in a while she will lay those instruments aside and pick up the rhumba box, a Haitian folk instrument, for a twanging, thumping percussion break.

In the early days of the civil rights struggle, when an interracial marriage was a strange and dangerous thing, David and Roselyn were deeply involved in voter registration drives in the South. They have lived in the ghettos of

David and Roselyn "tryin' to make a living"

Detroit and have even played on the street in that city. Their first streetsinging experience came out of desperation, when on the way to Miami their bus broke down in Louisiana and stranded them with no money for repairs. Since then they've "put in the hours," and their easeful confidence on the street comes from years of experience with all kinds of situations. Their year is divided between New Orleans and Los Angeles, and they earn most of their living on the street, playing only occasional nightclub or coffeehouse dates. "Why should we pay a big percentage to a manager and an agent and a club owner?" asks David.

A more tentative union, both musically and personally, is that of Edie O'Donnell and John D'Van. Edie prefers to be called Brooke ("Babbling Brooke," she giggles), and John calls himself Johnny Light. Sometimes they play and travel together, and sometimes their lives diverge into solos. Edie taught herself the Appalachian dulcimer about two years ago, and on the street she sits on a low stool, her many skirts spread around her, and sings traditional and modern folk songs in a high, thin soprano. When John joins her, he adds depth and volume with his voice and guitar.

When I asked Edie if she deliberately sings in a mountain voice, she was eager to please. "I *feel* like hill folks sometimes," she responded, "and I've listened to other people that do mountain music." But she was born in Ohio, and she and John now live in Detroit. They often visit New Orleans, where I met them. Her round, childish face with blue eyes under pale eyebrows beamed earnest goodwill as she talked about her music. "Anybody who plays a guitar has to prove themselves. But me—I'm just an amateur dulcimer player with an untrained voice. But I love to sing." It is hard to believe that Edie is thirty-three and has an eleven-year-old daughter.

"I enjoy life," she explained. "I raise plants and I weave

and I write poetry and I paint and I housekeep and chop wood to heat my house, and do whatever I can to just get by." Her relaxed and resourceful attitude toward life was demonstrated as the week wore on and the weather got colder. She added leotards and sweaters under her peasant blouse and yet another skirt or two to the motley patterns and colors hanging in a succession of hems to her ankles.

John has a more disciplined but an equally cheerful mind. He is very interested in the concept of networking, and has a vision of an interlocking communications structure that would link street people and other free souls. While in New Orleans he used his organizing skills to bring the performers together to talk about police harassment. Although they enjoy their music, it is not really central to them. Street music is a means to their life-style, not an end in itself. They inspired me with a nostalgia for the sixties. John and Edie are guileless and gentle people, hippies in the old style, with all their dreams of a world brotherhood of the good people still intact.

The cement that holds duos together is more often psychological than musical. A strange example is the team of Jingles and Frank. Both see themselves as wildly mismatched: "the odd couple of contemporary music," says their business card. They perceive Frank as a straight foil for Jingles's flamboyant image. To the nonstreet person, there is little difference except that Jingles dresses in costumes. Both are tall, thin, and craggy-nosed. Both play guitars and sing and are fanatical environment and food purists. Frank, however, came to the street from a promising law career, and at one time in his life Jingles *did* represent everything that attracted and frightened him from the free life he now leads. To Jingles, on the other hand, Frank represents the security of the straight world, and although they quarrel and part often, he is uneasy without him.

In performance Jingles is musically and visually domi-
nant—Frank is background. It is only after recovering
from the considerable impact of Jingles's wardrobe that
the listener can absorb his fine, strong voice and sure mu-
sicianship on the guitar. His closets are astonishing—racks
of satin pants in all colors, shirts of silk and lace and
sequins, jackets from Sergeant Pepper's Band or the age of
the cavalier, a swirling emerald-green satin cape, another
in eggplant velvet lined with red and yellow flowered silk,
drawers crammed with rainbow-hued scarfs and belts,
hats trimmed with ostrich plumes . . . And these are his
everyday clothes. It caused a great deal of merriment in
Venice last year when Jingles's picture appeared in a newspaper fashion spread about chic clothes for the beachfront.
"You should see me on Monday," he had told the reporter
with a straight face. "I dress like a stockbroker during the
week."

He says, "I dress up like nobody else. I dress up like my
mother never wanted me to dress." Jingles comes from a
Jewish professional family in Philadelphia; his father and
brothers are doctors. He was given his first guitar at his
bar mitzvah, and soon showed his talent by playing
his first gig at his grandfather's Golden Age club. But his
family's expectations and pressures became unbearable as
he grew up: "I was born to be a crazy person—couldn't
stay in high school, couldn't stay in jobs, couldn't stay in
the army." He left home, and for a long period in his life
was estranged from his family. During the sixties he sang
in Greenwich Village in nightclubs under the name Wild
Gypsy Jingles. Agents exploited his resemblance to the
then-popular Tiny Tim and encouraged him to outrageous
behavior onstage—throwing carrots and bells at the audience, dropping his pants, and flinging his long legs in
grotesque dances. Bohemian night life finally destroyed
his mental and physical health, and he came west to Cali-

fornia to heal. On the streets of Venice he found acceptance. "I conquered this town, didn't I?" he gloated. "I'm famous—a landmark!" But not rich. "I'm the poorest famous person you ever met," he often tells fans. "Jingles is a low-income superstar!"

Aside from his clothes, Jingles' schtick is bells. He has a huge collection of them: temple bells, bell rattles, and jinglers of all descriptions. During his finale—a thunderous rendition of Jingle Bells—he passes them out to a hand-picked selection of pretty volunteers ("The Bellettes"). Whenever the spirit moves him during his act or at parties or on the street, he distributes little bells on clips as a mark of his favor—to be "jingled" is a status symbol in Venice. He estimates that he has given out "maybe 150,000."

In spite of his thirty-two years, Jingles has a gangly, boyish demeanor that some women find attractive. Teeny-boppers, especially, cluster around him in adoring, giggling hordes, vying for his attention. He does his best to get around to them all, and falls in love at least twice a week. The pressures of adoration, however, as many other performers have found, can be overwhelming, even to an egoist like Jingles who refers to himself in the third person. One day he came home to find that a pretty fan had forced open his bathroom window, climbed in, and was sitting in the kitchen drinking coffee when he walked in the door. He called the police and had her taken away.

Triple relationships of long duration are as rare musically as in life, and it takes three individuals of extraordinary maturity to sustain a trio. The members of Allegra are such people. Anna Fessenden, Jack Werner, and Rick Mulcahy have a peaceful simplicity of manner that comes from knowing what is really important. Theirs is an examined life, and the decision to devote their talents to the street was made only after careful consideration. Jack and

Anna (who grew up as the daughter of a United Nations ambassador) have been together for eight years. They met in college and went on to teach theater arts at a university in Boston. They soon found themselves reaching for a simpler reality. Dropping out of the academic world, they took jobs working with their hands. Jack was a gardener, while Anna was a housekeeper. In the meantime, Rick had been traveling a similar road. From a career in children's theater and commercial art, he had come to dairy farming. The three met at a party and immediately discovered that their music-making and their life goals meshed. They came together more and more often to sing, and soon joined living arrangements.

One day they were harmonizing as they rode on the Boston subway, when a little old lady came up and gave them fifty cents. The gift brought them the realization that it might be possible to make a living with the music they all loved. Within four months they decided to try street-singing as a life. With typical careful planning, they all quit their jobs on Christmas Day 1978 and set out to travel the country for a year in search of the best places to perform. They went South "until it was warm enough to sit outside," spent two months in Key West, and then sampled the streetsinging climate across the nation. At the end of a year they had agreed that Boston and New Orleans were their places. "We like an old city where people are on foot, with winding streets closed off to traffic." They summer in Boston, from May to October, and winter in New Orleans.

To come across Allegra playing on those winding streets is like finding wildflowers growing in a parking lot. Their street style is unusual: They spread blankets on the pavement and sit in a triangle facing each other with their many musical instruments laid out around them. Anna, with her petite, rounded figure, high forehead, and small,

Allegra: Anna, Jack, and Rick

tip-tilted nose, is like a Victorian valentine in her flower-sprigged, long-skirted dress, and the men, in ruffled peasant shirts with their long hair tied neatly back, are almost as picturesque. As they tune up a crowd gathers, curious as to what kind of music will be produced.

This pregathering is part of the plan; it is important to Allegra to have this circle of bodies (which they call "the donut") as an acoustical container for their rather delicate sound. They play a variety of string and wind instruments. Rick is proficient on guitar, mandolin, banjo, recorder. Jack does recorder, autoharp, mandolin, jaw-harp, tambourine, Irish harp, and banjo. Anna plays all of the above plus clarinet, piano, ocarina, and she is learning the zither. They resist attempts to classify the style of their music, although it does lean toward Irish and American old-time traditional, Renaissance, spirituals, and madrigals. The album they cut and produced themselves has selections ranging from "Bile 'Em Cabbage Down" to a Bach lute prelude. Every week they try to learn a new piece, and Rick has just learned to read music, a skill that opens up the classics to them and makes arranging easier.

The members of Allegra are fond of elderly people, and feel that their gentle music has a special appeal to those between the ages of sixty and eighty, who are frightened by more boisterous performers. And the old people are fond of them, bringing them little gifts of food and trinkets. The trio's peaceful, loving air surrounds them with a protective aura, and they have never lacked for food or a place to stay in their travels. Several of their musical instruments were gifts from admirers, and in New Orleans a friend loans them a house to use during the winter. Content with the street as a stage, they have turned down offers from agents and nightclubs. "We never have and never will sell anybody's drinks," they say firmly. "The street is just the most beautiful place. Nobody stops unless they want to hear. And they're *so* quiet—they're not eating, they're not talking to each other, they're just giving us one hundred percent attention."

Other trios are not so peaceful, nor so content with the street. Unless three musicians share a life, it is almost impossible to survive solely on street earnings split in thirds, so most such groups are either supplementing their income or showcasing themselves with ambitions to move on to paid indoor performing. On the Air is a San Francisco swing trio that is on its way to someplace else. "We definitely don't plan to be on the street forever. It's a way to make money and practice our songs," said lead singer Ned Ripple. He and the other members of the group, Paul Gittelsohn and Pud Zippers, sing music from the late thirties. "We cats will swing for you," says their business card.

Authentically costumed in baggy pants with pleats, suspenders over colored shirts rolled above the elbow, saddle shoes, and sporty white billed caps, they sing in

On the Air at the Cannery

falsetto or tenor half-voices, putting in lots of jazzy hot licks on guitar, banjo, and bass. Their repertoire is culled from old records—reissues or collectors' items. Forties jazz is highly in demand in San Francisco: "We have to be on the ball, get those records quick," says Pud. Authentic period arrangements of numbers like "My Blue Heaven," "Have a Little Dream on Me," "Ragtime Cowboy Joe," "Choo Choo Boogie" ("our most contemporary song"), and "Who Put the Benzedrine in Mrs. Murphy's Ovaltine" have earned them a devoted following. The group was formed in spring of 1979. That summer they rehearsed six days a week while continuing to work at conventional jobs and playing regularly on the street and on the Cannery stage, and by the next spring they were successful nightclub entertainers.

Watching acts grow and develop over a period of time is one of the pleasures of being a street-performing aficionado. Slavin' David and His All Star Band is a group that has hit its stride only recently, although David has been playing guitar in Venice most of his life. A local homeboy, he was a Canaligator (the group started in the sixties by Hook and Butch Mudbone) and grew up among the winos and hippies of the oceanfront. For a long time the snarling anger of his performance drove audiences away. Not even incompetence alienates listeners the way hostility does. The situation fed on itself; although David is a good musician, the less money he got, the more insulting he became and the more unpleasant he was to watch. Suddenly at the end of summer 1979 his act began to improve. The shifting cast of musicians that made up the band settled down to Ramblin' Rick on guitar, Rockin' Billy Rizzi on string bass, and Ken Bowie on harmonicas, and David mellowed out as the take grew and his life got better. Now Slavin' and the band draw a raucous three-deep crowd every weekend. His anger has been plowed back into the music and gives it the excitement of suppressed violence. He describes it as "high-energy fifties rock, a few blues songs thrown in there, a couple of boogie tunes, shades of rockabilly . . ." When the music is really cooking, David will often explode into a frenetic dance. Crouched over the guitar with his soft leather cap pulled down over his eyes, he hops rapidly across the circle on one foot like a demented pelican, whirls around and around, and rolls over on his back with feet kicking in the air. I asked him about its origins: "I always was a good dancer. When I started getting heavily into performing out here it just came naturally. I copied Chuck Berry, the duck walk and all that, and I started getting my own moves. Sometimes I used to get real drunk and loose— I've been known to dip into the till a bit. I'd lose my inhibitions and start dancin' 'round with the guitar. I don't think about what I'm gonna do. I don't go home and practice steps in the mirror or anything." In spite of the excellence of his music, Slavin' claims "the only reason I play is to meet girls." He works hard at that objective, inviting women to

"Don't be shy—
Step up and say hi!"

and introducing himself publicly to any foxy lady in the front row.

Although performing groups composed of members of a family are a European tradition, in America such groups are rare on the streets. I encountered only the Wheland Brothers, preteen boys who play Irish music in Boston, and the Avila Family in Los Angeles. Mama and Papa Avila and their four children perform in a row standing at their long marimba, pounding away with padded mallets, and playing guitar or mandolin or violin or drums. Everybody does his bit, and the music that is produced is a big loud sound—Spanish, Mexican, and Anglo standards. To liven things up even more, the two pretty teen-age daughters have a variety of odd but spectacular specialties. Wearing slippers with mallets extending from the toes, one of the girls climbs up on a high chair and plays the marimba with her feet while the other stands behind and joins her in a two-handed solo on one violin, or uses a strand of her sister's hair for a violin bow. The oldest girl can play the mandolin with her mouth, and the smallest of the two little boys is held aloft by one foot by the father to play a xylophone on a high stand. But the moment that brings down the house is the drum solo banged out with fierce concentration and perfect tempo by the tiny five-year-old son. "It is good for families to do things together," said Mama. The Avilas were all taught by the father, who was already a professional musician when he came to the United States in 1954. They are highly in demand for banquets and parties in Spanish-speaking East Los Angeles, and they play regularly on the street at Redondo Pier and Chinatown. All the Avilas are busy with work and school during the week, and the extra money they earn with their music is being used for the daughters' college education.

As I talked to musical groups on the streets I discovered a network of people involved in re-creating old-time American music. They are careful to distinguish it from bluegrass, although it sounds similar, to the unsophisticated ear. Old-time music is pre-1930s dance tunes—reels, squares, contras—with English, Irish, and Scottish origins. It developed in the Appalachians, and much of it was preserved on records in the twenties and thirties. Unlike bluegrass, this old-time music consists of a single melody. The devotees of this music learn it from old records, each other, and the few surviving elders who can reproduce the dance tunes of their youth. In New York the old-time music people gather at the Eagle Tavern, where musicians can jam together and find others to join in a band. Since there is a standard repertoire, almost any old-time musician can sit in with others from anywhere in the country —"a lot of the tunes we play are common knowledge," said Jack Hirschorn of the Color by Number String Band. "I can meet people from California, Utah, New Mexico, who know the same tunes." Jack and his group once invited everyone they knew who played old-time music to a street-corner performance in honor of a friend's birthday. Eighteen people showed up and joined in. The police were stunned, said Jack, and only after several numbers did they collect themselves enough to come up and whisper to the leader, "Go somewhere else."

In Boston I visited young old-time musicians Susan Malspies and Bruce Mandaro in their rambling Forest Hills apartment. Sitting at a sturdy round oak table in their big kitchen, we looked out at the grassy yard with tangles of flowers and listened to tapes of Otis Grove, their musical group. A tiger cat purred at our feet, and coffee perked in an enamel pot while Susan sliced homemade pumpkin bread. Tossing her long braid over her shoulder, she explained that while in summer she and Bruce make their whole living on the street, in winter they supplement their income, rather than leave Boston, with other jobs. Bruce plays with country and rock and roll bands, and Susan does crafts and teaches guitar to children. Otis Grove is a flexible group. In addition to Susan on guitar and Bruce on mandolin, they are joined by Marsha the fiddle player and sometimes a banjo or a bass or another guitar.

An extra member that sits in with them from time to time is a bones player—called, inevitably, Mr. Bones. He is a popular addition to bands, because this ancient form of percussion is fun to watch and a crowd-pleaser on the street. As Susan described Mr. Bones, I was struck with the similarity to Hank Kahn, the "Mr. Bones" of the West Coast. Susan's Mr. Bones is an older man who has a full-time job selling insulation, his trade for twenty-five years. A loner, he sits in with various bands and plays with country and even punk groups. Hank Kahn is also an older man with a straight job—a quality control engineer. "I play the bones for a living, and am a quality control engineer for money," he says. He has just come back from a trip around the world, where he played with bands in pubs in Ireland and was auditioned in Egypt by Anwar Sadat's sister, who asked him to play on TV with Arabic music. Hank can manage up to four objects—bones, clappers, even salad spoons in a pinch—in one hand, and is in demand as a street performer with all kinds of music.

Old Mother Logo is an all-woman string band that learned its skills on the street and is now working with an agent for indoor gigs. The group was founded three years ago when Monika White, who had played banjo and sung old-timey songs for five years for friends, was invited to do a performance at Magic Mountain Amusement Park. Terrified of her first stage appearance, she asked friends Dodi Klein and Nel Rosenblum to play along. The group named itself just before they went onstage from the title of one of the five songs they knew in common. The debut was a success. They practiced, improved, and began to play on Venice Beach to rehearse with an audience. "Any money at all was a bonus," said Monika. They used their street-performing experience to learn "to play loud and sing loud. It takes self-confidence to throw it out." They developed an instinct for "what holds people" and found it "an opportunity to test material and ourselves. It was great training." After several months of street experience they bought a string bass and cajoled Monika's twin sister Gitta Morris into learning to play it. At a Christmas festival they found lead singer and bones player Piper Heisig. By this time the group had become professional enough to attract the attention of manager Gee Martin, who took them under his wing and got them a summer job at Knott's Berry Farm, a Western-theme amusement park near Los Angeles. The first thing he did was make them promise not to play anymore on the street. "Why buy the cow when you can get the milk free?" he asked. The group will soon make the commitment to full-time music; they are waiting only for fiddler Nel, who is fifty-four, to retire from her job as a bilingual teacher, and for Monika to complete her Ph.D. in gerontology.

Old-time music groups are primarily motivated by their love of the music, and the street earnings are secondary. The groups change and shift in composition as musicians come and go. A band may play for a while on one corner, lose a few members and be joined by others, and later decide to walk down a few blocks and combine forces with another group. The spare change that lands in the guitar case is only enough for beer and gas when it is split five or six ways. Only the most hard-working and ascetic musicians can live off the street as part of a band. It is entirely possible to finance a trip from street money, however, if the group is small, eats light, and sleeps in the van. The Down Home String Band are five young fishermen from the San Juan Islands in Washington who during the off-season pack up their van and their instruments and tour the United States playing for their supper. The Water Street Boys Jug Band is a colorfully dressed and very motley group of ten friends from upper New York State, who financed a trip to the Mardi Gras with their zany, foot-stomping renditions on kazoo, spoons, washboard, washtub bass, trombone, and the more usual guitar, banjo, harmonica, and fiddle.

Lovers and performers of bluegrass music also have a

network across the country, a circuit of festivals and get-togethers. Bluegrass is a regional style characterized by high tenor harmonies, a picking-style banjo, a structure based on solos for each performer, and a driving, overriding energy. It is a type of music that works extremely well on the street. And bluegrass is loud; it makes up in volume what it lacks in subtlety—an advantage outdoors. The best in New York is said to be the Seldom Seen Band (but true to their name, I missed them). Others are Snooze-u-lose in San Francisco and Hayfever in Westwood Village.

Dixieland bands, too, are highly appropriate for the street. We have already met Scotty Hill, leader of the Original French Market Jazz Band. Scotty spent some time in San Francisco several years ago, and was taught street skills by John Stafford, whose Bourbon Street Irregulars served their apprenticeship on the street and are now respectably employed at the St. Francis Hotel. Scotty's band has both black and white members, but he feels that their most unusual feature is that they are young. "For a whole generation black people felt this music was old-fashioned," he said. Only recently have young musicians been returning to the tradition of Dixieland. There are six men in Scotty's band; the structure is loose. "Musicians come and musicians go," he says with a shrug. Scotty feels that the challenge is to breathe life and spirit into music that is very old. "Tourists think of little old middle-aged men in straw hats and striped jackets playing this real fast, frantic, stiff music, but there's a lot more to it than that. Bourbon Street has reduced it to formula music." The old New Orleans jazz was dance-hall music, music of celebration. On the street they "get closer to the old idea of what the music is about"—people clap, dance, enjoy themselves freely. When he first began playing in the streets he was very shy about it. "I thought it was one step from begging. But I soon realized it was more giving than receiving." Each week the band plays two or three club gigs and performs on the street twice. They think of their street earnings as a subsidy. Scotty's band has been up and it's been down. About 1976 they were arrested, and the resulting brouhaha led to a moratorium on street performing in New Orleans for almost a year, but at about the same time they were also discovered by RCA and taken to New York to cut a record.

Classical music can have great serendipity in the right setting on the street. Barbara Mason of the French Quarter Chamber Music Gang says, "We've done a beautiful, beautiful concert in the evening in summertime by the cathedral, and when it's quiet in the Square at night like that you can just hear it and it's really like a chamber concert." However, the street is often too impatient an environment for the enjoyment of more demanding music. Classical groups that make a living or even play regularly on the street are extremely rare. There are a number of groups in New York whose members are classically trained but who supplement their street repertoire with Scott Joplin, the Beatles, John Philip Sousa, or other more crowd-pleasing selections. Mozart on Fifth is a clarinet, oboe, bassoon combination that dresses in satin knee-britches and velvet coats and hangs out on Fifth Avenue, the Upper West Side, and the Staten Island Ferry. They play Mozart, but also ragtime and other styles. More classical groups are the Linden Woodwind Quartet, the Olympic Brass Quintet, the Riverside Brass Quintet, and the Waldo Park Brass Players, who provide an open chair for all out-of-work brass musicians. (Waldo Park, its members explain, does not appear on the city map—it is a state of mind.)

JOSIAH IN GRIEF

The tall louvered doors of the apartment next door were ajar when we came home through the trash-strewn streets of Mardi Gras evening. We leaned across the worn concrete stoop and called in, "Hey Josiah! Happy Mardi Gras, man! Did you have a good one?"

He stood, uncertain and disconsolate, in the middle of the room, tall and spare in his faded jeans. "Well, yeah, I made a hundred and fifty dollars this week . . ." he said in his soft North Carolina voice. His long, sensitive hands hung empty at his sides, and he moved them spasmodically. "But tonight somebody stole my fiddle—I looked everywhere and I can't find it and I don't know where to look anymore! It's gone, man, it's gone!" His voice broke and his grief filled the room.

I reached out to hug him close and comfort him, and he clung tightly to me like a lost child. "It was a hundred and fifty years old, my fiddle, and it was handmade! I've had it all these years when I was travelin' 'round. And me and the group were just getting it to where the music was working just right, and now what am I goin' to do! Oh!" He laid his head on my shoulder and I rocked him and stroked his back.

I thought of all the times I had seen Josiah and the other two members of Hickory Stick playing their hearts out on the street that Mardi Gras week—on the steps of the public buildings on Royal, nodding cheerfully to me in the midst of a dance tune, in shop alcoves and on street corners, and once late at night on the banks of the beer-sodden river of humanity that was Bourbon Street, when the temperature was 38 and we had our hands deep in our pockets to keep warm. There they stood with their cold fingers flying on the strings to make that fine old American music, worn spare and true with the years. But most of all I remembered Josiah at an all-night jam upstairs. He had been slumped down on the couch, lying almost flat, nearly asleep, but still playing quietly. His fiddle lay cradled on his chest. I had watched the delicacy of his fingers moving the bow, seen the strings respond in love to his touch, and known for certain that for this man his violin was more than the instrument of his survival, the means of his living, more than a companion and a lover. For Josiah his fiddle was part of his body. And now it was gone.

But he is a survivor, this North Carolina music man, and he has grown strong from the years of this hard life he has chosen. And he is a seeker after truth, who has long since left all anger behind him. He has none now for the thief who has deprived him. "A lot of people played that fiddle before me," he says, lifting his head from my shoulder. "There was a lot of music on that old fiddle!" I brush the tears from his cheeks with the palm of my hand, and I see that there are a few white hairs in his neatly trimmed beard. A tremulous smile lights up his face. "I tell you what, I hope whoever stole it just plays the shit out of it!" Then his loss overcomes him again, and he moans softly. "My fiddle. Oh, my good old fiddle."

JUGGLERS

"Do you think juggling's a mere trick?" the little man asked, sounding wounded. "An amusement for the gapers? A means of picking up a crown or two at a provincial carnival? It is all those things, yes, but first it is a way of life, friend, a creed, a species of worship."

—Robert Silverberg,
Lord Valentine's Castle

Fire flies above the heads of the evening strollers in Westwood Village—sticks of flame end over end, against the dark sky. Pushing through to the front of the crowd, I see a young juggler, broad-shouldered and naked to the waist, his long blond hair lashing about his intent face as he hurls torches into the air with fierce concentration. He catches the three flaming rods, extinguishes them, and seizes a long curving scythe. He balances it on his chin, and I am intensely aware that one error will send the keen rounded edge slicing down between his legs. Reaching for a machete and a meat cleaver, he sends the blades flashing and whirling, and then climaxes his act by heaving three bowling balls into the air in a lumbering, straining defiance of gravity. The audience, who has watched this flirtation with danger from a respectful distance, suddenly

Jim Cappe defies gravity with three bowling balls

finds that they have been drawn into the risks—the jug-gler climbs up on a tall, thin unicycle and lowers a black blindfold over his eyes. "Now, I can't see you," he warns in a harsh, strident voice, "so if I come at you, get out of the way!" Then, playing a harmonica and a concertina, he careens wildly around the edge of the circle as the crowd shrieks and scrambles in delighted alarm.

This fierce young showman is Jim Cappe, and his obses-sion with self-risk (he also does Houdini chain escapes underwater) has made his juggling act one of the most dynamic on the street. Jim has been a self-supporting busker since the age of eleven, when he was entranced by watching a comedian perform on the streets of his native Sausalito and set out to teach himself juggling. As a young teen-ager he traveled in Europe and juggled on the street and in nightclubs, working at the Moulin Rouge in Paris when he was only fourteen. Now, at eighteen, he is a hard-shelled professional and a regular performer in both Northern and Southern California.

Jim is an example of the renaissance of virtuoso juggling that is one of the delights of the new street theater. Throughout the history of civilization, wherever people have thronged the streets, wherever popular theater has flourished, there have been jugglers. In America, juggling was a staple of the vaudeville stage—W. C. Fields, for in-stance, got his start by using it as a background for his throwaway monologues.

In spite of its persistent fascination in the history of theater, juggling has always been something of a show business stepchild. Although it takes years of practice to acquire the techniques and to put together a polished act, jugglers have never been regarded as fine artists. They share in that hoary theater curse, "May all your children be acrobats!"

Today, with the emergence of the street scene, jugglers

have come into their own. During the recent American Dark Ages of live popular theater it survived in circuses and carnivals, but now it has reappeared on the streets in brilliant new guise, with breathtaking techniques and split-second showmanship. Acts such as the Fantasy Jugglers of Boston—whose intricately choreographed juggling suite with percussion has form, structure, and emotional subtlety—have lifted the once-humble craft of tossing-up to high art, or at least high theater.

The new opportunities for jugglers to be seen and to make a living on the street have led to this flowering, but also the resulting competition and camaraderie have inspired new heights of skill. Jugglers are a close fraternity; they know each other all over the country, and they agree on who is good, who is getting better, and who is best of all. Enrico Ristelli, they will tell you, was the best juggler of all time. Nick Lucas of the Ice Capades is the best in the United States, and Ed Jackman won at IJA last year. The International Jugglers' Association holds an annual convention at which they all come together to share and compare and to compete among themselves for the distinction of being judged best by their peers. The IJA is no little Sunday School picnic; it now has over a thousand paid members, and the gathering is impressive.

A reservoir of juggling talent has developed on college and high school campuses during the last several years, as it became a fad among athletes on the West Coast. "At first it sort of came out of the sixties consciousness," said Kit Trueblood of the Juggling Mizmos. The intense concentration was equated with the mind-transforming effects of meditation. Later it "became an athletic, white, middle-class, suburban fad. Now it's a jock thing."

The good street juggler must first of all be a trained athlete, with pinpoint concentration and lightning reflexes. Most will refuse alcohol for hours before a performance,

Gary Calder practices
at Fisherman's Wharf

and constant practice is a necessary discipline. But technique is only the starting point for a good show. Virtuosity must be showcased with patter, flair, costumes, pacing to hold the restless street-audience's interest. And this is what distinguishes the art of juggling from the sport of juggling.

The knack of making a trick *look* hard is an invaluable asset; without it even an accomplished juggler will leave an audience unmoved. Few laypersons are able to distinguish a really difficult stunt from a merely showy one; juggler after juggler told me that his hardest trick was the neck catch, yet it is relatively unimpressive to watch and seldom draws a big hand. Rawd Holbrook of the Fantasy Jugglers said, "You can really tell the difference between people that practice juggling and are just very good jugglers, and people that can make you *think* that they're good jugglers. That's the whole name of the game."

"Gary Calder is the best juggler in town—technically," said his colleagues in San Francisco. Gary's technique is dazzling—he almost never misses, and he can control six (or sometimes seven) rings in the air and then catch them one after the other around his neck. But his patter is a bit tentative and unsure, and his act lacks cohesiveness. Gary is working on his deficiencies and has improved enormously in the time he has been in San Francisco. "The first street performing I did was nine months ago," he told me. "I was terrible at first—argh! The audience walked away. I was doing the same tricks, basically, but they still walked away. People don't care about tricks unless you make them care somehow."

Gary's willingness to work on self-improvement is characteristic. His life contradicts the stereotype of the indolent, self-indulgent busker who presumably is on the street because he is too lazy to get a job. Gary planned his career as a street juggler with all the long-term self-discipline of a Ph.D. candidate or a corporate management trainee. He has been preparing to be a busker for five years. "I'm very responsible and organized and directed," he says.

Very early in his college years he was introduced to the basics of juggling: cascades (in which the balls travel in an arc from hand to hand) and showers (in which the balls are tossed in a circle). He played with the two techniques until he had mastered them, and then put it down because he had never seen a professional juggler and thought that that was all there was to it. Three years later he saw his first juggling performance and all of a sudden realized there was a lot more. He began to practice again, increased his skills, and went to the IJA convention, where he "was totally amazed—my knowledge increased by tenfold." He was exposed to passing with clubs and balls, the bongo boards, cigar boxes, the devil sticks, the diablo, unicycle riding . . . He went home on fire with ambition, arranged his job hours so that he could practice three to seven hours a day in a high-ceilinged dormitory lounge, and stuck to this demanding schedule for two years. When he had achieved technical excellence, he "retired" from his job and chose Eugene, Oregon, as a nonthreatening town to begin his street career. Almost immediately he realized that his natural shyness was a handicap, and that he needed more training, this time in performance skills. Undeterred, he joined a theater group that provided a secure atmosphere for learning, and worked with them for two and a half years.

At last he felt ready for the big time. Almost as soon as he appeared on the street in San Francisco he was offered a place at Pier 39, where he is now scheduled five days a week in the prime late afternoon and early evening hours. Watching other performers to improve his crowd control and patter has been a postgraduate study for Gary, and at the same time he continues to grow in mastery of juggling

techniques. Currently he is learning to control five clubs—
"the hardest thing I've worked on. Everything has to be
just perfect." Sometimes he practices in front of a mirror
to achieve symmetry: "You have to get the feel of what
it's like to have your hands just even," he said, demon-
strating, his blond hair blowing in the ocean breeze and
his good-looking boyish face intent.

Jugglers have a full-time commitment to the streets that
is different in kind from that of musicians, for several reasons. First, to be even competent, a performing juggler
must maintain a dedication to constant physical self-
discipline and practice; there is no room for the casual
dilettante or the part-time hobbyist. Second, it is easier
for a juggler to draw a crowd and make a living on the
streets—a musician may be heard but ignored, while it is
harder for the passerby to walk past the visual excitement
of juggling without stopping for at least a few minutes.
Unlike music, the dynamics of a good juggling act work
up to a psychologically advantageous moment for money-
collecting: There are a beginning, a middle, and a boffo
finish. The audience is held and entertained for twenty
minutes and feels that they have had their money's worth.
Third, and most important, jugglers are committed to the
street because there is no place else for them to go. Musicians can aspire to nightclubs, concerts, recording dates.
Jugglers have only the circus, and that, I found to my surprise, is not considered the big time. When the Fly by
Night Jugglers, a very young four-man San Francisco
group, told me they had just signed clown contracts with
Ringling, I congratulated them, but later other performers
said, "It's okay for them—they're just out of high school
and it will be fun for them for a season. But circus only
pays minimum wage and I'm trying to make a decent
living."

Many street jugglers, then, are "lifers" (as Paul Levey

termed it): men who feel that for them the street is the best of all possible theatrical worlds and who are content to stay there. Many of them have developed coherent philosophies of busking. Ray Jason, dean of San Francisco street performers, is one of the most articulate. In *Air California* Magazine he said: "Street performing is pointing in a new direction, toward a more humane, personal-scale form of entertainment that is affordable by everyone, that transcends racial or ethnic barriers, that can be relaxed, topical and provocative. It fits into the whole 'Small is beautiful' concept—street performing is a more exhilarating experience because only two hundred have been able to share it, and so there is a stronger common bond."

Ray was the first street juggler in San Francisco, and probably in the United States ("Nine years and twenty-eight days," he said proudly). His years of experience have given him a relaxed, natural manner onstage that puts audiences at ease. Ray juggles torches lying flat on his back, and then leaps straight up for a flashy finish. He tosses four basketballs fifty feet up to cries of "Higher!" from the audience. He masters five balls and catches one on the back of his neck and—unbelievably—throws it ten times in the air using only his deltoid muscles, and he winds up with his signature trick—two hatchets and an apple, which he eats on the fly while riding a unicycle. His patter is glib and amusing, and only on a second hearing does it become apparent that it is rehearsed and not spontaneous.

Ray shows off his well-developed shoulders in sleeveless leotards (even in the coldest weather), and his athlete's body is surprisingly graceful in action as he lunges and pirouettes. He is constantly working to improve his act, and this year has been learning tap-dancing to add to his juggles.

A generous and sweet-natured person, Ray puts together an annual free stage show on his street anniversary
to thank the people of San Francisco for supporting street
performers. It is financed by donation and Ray's own
pocket, and highlights the best busking of the year. The
last three of these shows have been videotaped and shown
as television specials.

In spite of the fact that he is almost a San Francisco in-
stitution, Ray Jason has been hauled off to jail for street
performing three times. But he has never had to stay in the
tank overnight, he points out, because he always goes out
onto the street prepared for the worst; he carries a dime in
each sock and the phone number of a good bailbondsman,
and cards with the names and phone numbers of three
friends to distribute to the crowd as he is taken away. On
his first bust he had a hard time convincing his fellow jail-
birds of his real occupation: "In those days I wore all black:
turtleneck with long sleeves, black pants, and black belt. So
I'm in the holding cell with these three other prisoners and
they say to me, 'What're you in here for?' (Everybody
swaps tales, you know—you got a grand larceny in there,
an assault and battery . . .) So I go 'Well, I'm in here for
juggling.'

" '*Juggling?*' So they take a look at me, and I'm dressed
in this all black outfit with an athletic build, and they say,
'C'mon, now, we've been around the block! We know a
goddamn cat burglar when we see one!' "

Edward Jackman is another of the best street jugglers.
For the last three years he has won the IJA competition,
and onstage he has presence, timing, and a masterful line
of patter to frame his repertoire of breathtaking tricks. Ed
looks like an athletic, all-American pixie, with a wicked
crooked grin and sardonic eyebrows that nearly meet over
his nose, topped by a curly mop of hair. He and his part-

ner, Daniel Rosen, who is only sixteen, have worked Washington Square in New York and are now scraping by on the weekend-only street environment of Los Angeles.

A close look at Ed's patter discloses some principles. First of all, he acknowledges the audience and establishes rapport and expectations: "Hello, everybody!" he says simply, after drawing a crowd with a three-ball juggle, "my name is Edward Jackman and I am—as you may have noticed—a juggler. Now before I start my show, let me ask you to move closer . . ." Then he uses the patter for continuity, tying together a string of tricks on the devil sticks with a story about the Emperor of China, who was forced by a curse to master them. "He learned the two-handed helicopter spin—the one-handed helicopter spin— he learned to do it under his legs—behind his back (behind his wife's back, too—he was a fun guy!)—and all sorts of nifty little things. But there was one trick the Emperor couldn't do, and that goes something like this"—and he flings a stick spinning high in the air for a spectacular finish. His club routine is presented as "tricks Enrico Ristelli used to do" ("Wow, was he ever good!") and "tricks even Enrico Ristelli couldn't do." He builds anticipation for a difficult pass by working up to it, doing first a one-club pirouette, then topping it with a two-club pirouette. To go straight on to a three-club pirouette from this point would be repetitive, and although the trick is very showy, it would be predictable. So Ed varies his patter slightly, and announcing the pirouette with three clubs, he then fakes it by turning without tossing. The audience laughs, and is half-convinced that the trick is not possible. Now, having laid down a nice blend of doubt and expectation, he finally does the pass—three times—and earns a wild burst of applause. Approaching his finale, he says, "I want you all to take both hands out of your pockets! Take both hands out of your friends' pockets, too! And everybody make a drum roll like this!" (He bends forward and slaps his thighs rapidly.) "Everybody! Now, are we ready?" (They shout "Yeah!") People come running from blocks away to see what all the noise is about, and Ed does a three-club juggle high in the air and somersaults forward under it for a perfect catch.

The possibilities for patter and tricks are doubled when Ed works with his partner, Daniel. At one point the two of them stage an argument over a cap, snatching it back and forth from each other's heads while walking in and out of a three-club juggle. The words in their act are as carefully rehearsed as the tricks; they speak some lines in unison, others alternating in a rapid-fire dialog. For their double finale they use the principle of doubt and expectation neatly, as Ed tries to add two fallen clubs into the six that are already flying between them. He tries and misses, tries and misses, until the audience is on the verge of feeling sorry for them, even though they suspect the miss is deliberate. At last Ed relieves the tension by scooping up both clubs easily, and ends by leaping high and catching the last toss triumphantly between his knees.

A most important use for patter is to cover a mistake. Every juggler drops occasionally, and it is crucial to maintain the audience's respect and sympathy but not to let it turn to pity for the error. Most jugglers respond to this psychological dilemma by instinctively reaching for a laugh and then repeating the trick. On the rare instances when Ed misses his catch after the forward roll, he seizes a club angrily and says to it, "You missed, you dummy!" Some jugglers point off into the distance and shout, "Look over there!" while they recover a fallen piece. Others make jokes about "floor juggling" or cry, "Hey, audience-participation time!" as a ball bounces off into the crowd. Jim Cappe, with typical fierceness, glares at the crowd and dares them to notice, while Butterfly says with gruff mock dignity, "Don't applaud—I don't need your pity!"—a line that is so close to the emotional reality that it draws a startled laugh every time.

Other two-man teams use the principles of patter in ways suited to their own stage personas. Tall Kit True-blood and short Fred Anderson of the Juggling Mizmos do a cap-passing routine that is comical because of the difference in their heights. They involve the audience quite elaborately by choosing four small children, lining them up with great suspense, warning them to hold *very* still ("Now pull in your noses!"), and juggling clubs just inches past their heads. Berkeley Jugglers Shawn Haines and Dave Gregory build their patter around the difference in their ages: Shawn is twenty-two while Dave is fourteen but looks ten. As Dave throws torches under his leg, he muses, "I'd hate to lose my equipment before I had a chance to test it!" At the climax of their act, when he has been hoisted with great difficulty to Shawn's shoulders and is preparing to juggle two huge machetes and a carrot, he suddenly crosses his legs and whines, "I have to go to the bathroom!"

A few acts, like the Fantasy Jugglers, dispense with patter entirely and use music or percussion to anticipate, underscore, and unify the passes. Dario and Olof are a successful Boston team of juggler and drummer. They met at the Modern Theater in Boston, where Dario was taking a class in mime and Olof was plastering and doing sets. One day Olof had taken his drums outside to practice during a break in the work, and Dario began fooling around with his juggling balls. He described the moment of realization: "We were getting into what we were doing—I was juggling away, and Olof was playing with his eyes closed, and I look up and there's *hundreds* of people watching! That's when we realized we had something." It is true that Olof's congas add an emotional dimension in a minor, almost ominous, mode. This sense of mystery is especially appropriate for Dario's performance, because he combines juggling with magic. For openers he often does a rainbow cloud: Throwing back his head, he turns his tall, thin body slowly as a stream of colored paper tape emerges from his mouth and soars straight up into the air for fifty feet, to hang curving and floating in the wind. His juggling is superbly controlled: He performs a cigar-box routine, learned from an ancient W. C. Fields film, that leads up to a tower of boxes balanced on his chin, and he climaxes his act with a forehead catch that he rolls over his head to the back of his neck and then flips back up into a juggle. Both men are serious professionals. They work regularly at Quincy Market and other outdoor fairs, festivals, parties, and they rehearse for long hours, refining nuances of their act. They have considerable money invested in their equipment, and they are meticulous about costuming and grooming. Olof is the conscientious single parent of a seven-year-old son, who brings his friends proudly to watch Daddy street performing.

The combination of juggling and magic is a historical one, going back to the jongleurs. Other theatrical arts also mix well with the balls and clubs. Mime and juggling is another natural pairing. And a few street comedians have found that juggling can be played entirely for laughs.

Sean Morey, who has recently made a name for himself on television, had a street repertoire of fast political juggles: the Jimmy Carter left-wing pass—and the right-wing pass (with a beatific grin), the corporation one-hand grab (mutters of "Gimme, gimme, gimme"), the FBI surveillance juggle (with alternate balls held to his ear), the China drop (Taiwan goes bouncing off into the crowd), the Sky Lab (one ball bounces off his head), the Watergate ("You take it"—"No, you take it"), the Richard Nixon (a tricky faked behind-the-back pass), and, of course, the Gerald

Ford, in which balls go flying off in all directions from his fumbling fingers and flailing elbows. (After watching Sean in Los Angeles, I was astonished to see this same routine being performed by Marc Wiener at the foot of the Metropolitan Museum steps in New York. He and Sean were once partners, he explained later, and had evolved the political juggles together.) Sean doesn't limit himself to tossing balls and clubs; he ends his street act by juggling a rubber chicken, a head of cabbage, and an M&M; on his last pass he catches the candy in his mouth. (On the opposite coast, Marc also catches the M&M, but, being a health food enthusiast, he then spits it out.) The climactic moment in this gallery of strange-object juggling comes when Sean announces, "For my last act I will juggle a fifty-dollar bill, a pubic hair, and a half ounce of cocaine. Donations of these objects will now be accepted from the audience."

San Francisco comedian Mike Davis uses juggling and magic as a frame for a droll, scatology-tinged routine that leaves the audience delighted but a bit nauseated. Drawing a crowd with card tricks delivered in a lazy W. C. Fields drawl, he holds them spellbound through a disappearing toilet-paper trick, knife juggling, and "the Ping-Pong balls of death" that pop wetly out of his mouth to bounce into the crowd, where they are usually caught and returned by small boys ("Eeyuh!" grimaces Mike). "May I borrow your cigarette?" he asks a smoker in the audience, then shoves the unlit end up his own nostril, where it hangs obscenely. He hands it back, and its owner recoils, giving Mike his cue to observe, "*Now* he's worried about his health!" As Mike works, the stage around him becomes littered with wads of toilet paper and vegetable debris. He tests his knives by whacking up carrots in midair, then proves the weight of a bowling ball by dropping it heavily into a carrot smash. His final trick is a triumph of untidiness. Juggling the bowling ball, an apple, and an egg, he takes huge bites out of the apple as it juggles past, until his mouth is bulging. The spectators, especially the small children, laugh. Then he misses and bites the egg, shattering it slimily over his chin. The laugh builds, and there are shrieks of disgust. The yolk drips off onto his ruffled shirt front and he stands in mock dismay and slowly opens his mouth to disgorge chewed apple over his chest to mix with the strings of raw egg—and the audience screams and howls in appalled hilarity. Later, as he was sweeping up after the show, he told me, "God, I hate doing that! My laundry bills are enormous; I use up fourteen shirts a week. But it gets such a big laugh that I'm stuck with it."

One of the best comedian-jugglers is Robert Armstrong Nelson III, known as the Butterfly Man. With his impeccable timing and enormous onstage magnetism he was born to be a clown, but only realized it a little over two years ago. A son of a Nobel prize winner and a former scientist himself, Butterfly is a completely happy man in his new life. Although he has worked diligently on perfecting every moment of his act and has the respect and admiration of other performers, he is still a bit uncertain about whether he has earned his sudden show business success. With modesty and wonder, he told me the story of his transformation from academic scientist to street juggler.

BUTTERFLY'S METAMORPHOSIS

The Butterfly Man is getting ready for a show at Pier 39, laying out his clubs and torches, his unicycle and diablo sticks, in patterns as precise as the preparation for the Japanese tea ceremony. He sets out a long-stemmed red rosebud in a vase, steps back to look at the effect, and comes down from the stage to sit with me on a bench. The carousel plays in the distance, and seagulls shriek overhead. He begins his story immediately, without preliminaries, speaking earnestly, as if he has thought about it a lot.

"Four years ago I was a research assistant at Vanderbilt University in the Department of Clinical Pharmacology. I did research on heart drugs—basically I was a test tube twiddler. But I wasn't happy with what I was doing; it wasn't enough creative outlet for me. So I said to myself, 'I'd like to give juggling a try. And performing.' (I wasn't a performer at the time; I had simply juggled to music and thought of taking it to different places.) Well, when I got a chance to be a juggling clown for four months at Opryland, U.S.A., I took it. It was a big decision to do that because I had a very stable, secure position and—you know, you work your way up the ladder. But I said, 'Okay, if it fails and I can't make my living as a juggler, I can always go back.'

"Sure enough, as soon as the Opryland job ended I was left without anything. I said, 'Okay, I'm going to hold out for a couple of weeks.' The next day I got called to juggle with a magic show. I put together about twenty minutes of juggling to music, no talking involved; that kept me going for a while. It got to be around December, and I had done maybe birthday parties and a few things in between, just enough to stay alive, pay my rent, pay my bills—I didn't have a lot of extra capital; it was just barely survival. And then I didn't get any more calls. For anything. It was wintertime in Nashville, and people just weren't hiring a juggler, so I spent almost five weeks without any income at all. I was hungry; I ate oatmeal.

"All of a sudden I began to hear about New Orleans and Mardi Gras. I knew that people had done tip acts down there, so I said, 'I wonder if I could go down there and pass my hat?' Now, I'd never done street performing before. I couldn't bring my music because I was going to be on the street, and I was going to have to say something while I juggled. I said, 'Okay, I'm going to go down and give it a try!' When I got there, I walked out on the street with all my juggling stuff and set it out. A few people gathered around just to look at it, saying, 'Well, what's going to go on here?' I was wearing my gold and red satin court jester outfit. I started juggling, and—didn't really know what to say. I didn't really do bad, but it wasn't cohesive. A couple of people threw a couple of quarters. It really didn't work at all, and I was very depressed.

"So I packed all my stuff up and I walked across to the other side of the street, across from the Café du Monde to the center of Jackson Square. Now, something about Jackson Square is magical! It's quiet because you don't have the traffic going by; it's a nice space for people to stop; it's a large area. . . . Well, I did my second show and there—it worked! I just started talking about anything that came into my head while I was juggling—the book I was reading, Carlos Casteneda, the tunnel, how I was locked in my garage—anything at all, I just threw it out! I got a few laughs, went on to the next thing, finished off, put a fire chief's hat on my head and did fire and ate the fire at the very end and said, 'Thank you very much.' The people put money in my hat, and I was flabbergasted. I did it again, and again.

"It got to be dark. I packed my stuff and said, 'That's

it for me today'—I was tired. I had done maybe five, six shows. So I went home. I was staying with the family of a friend of mine, an elderly lady and gentleman. They said, 'How did you do today?' I said, 'Gee, I really don't know. Got all the money in my knapsack. Let's put it on the table—would you help me count it?' I figured I'd made fifty bucks or something. Well, it turned out I'd made a hundred and fifty dollars! I was blown away! A hundred and fifty dollars for a person that was dead broke and had to borrow five dollars just for gas money to get into town! They were very impressed. They helped me count it all, put it in little coin rolls and things . . . The next day I went out at ten o'clock in the morning and worked very, very hard all day, and did twice as good. And I just kept doing it for another day and a half. I put all the money in a paper sack, and I went back to Nashville; I paid my rent, bought some groceries, paid my bills, and I had just enough to survive for a little while.

"It started to be springtime, and I began to get little jobs again: birthday parties, private parties, street gigs . . . I knew that the juggling convention was going to happen in Eugene, Oregon, in July, so I said to myself, 'Well, I want to go to it. It's very important to me professionally, because you see a whole bunch of new tricks and you get a lot of new ideas and you meet all the other professional jugglers.' So I went to the bars around town at nighttime, and I juggled my torches on the outside of the bar. I had to get the money to go somehow. People weren't highly receptive to a person doing tip acts in Nashville, Tennessee. I'd go inside and I'd juggle to music—whatever was on the jukebox, or sometimes a guitar player would be there. That was my magic. That's what I could do that nobody else could do—make music visual. Then I'd pass the hat or just stand there if anybody wanted to put anything in. I wouldn't make a lot—sometimes only eight dollars, sometimes ten . . . Then I'd leave, and I'd go into another place and do it again. I made just enough money doing that to go to Eugene for the convention."

(Butterfly goes on to tell about how on the way home from the convention—where he had learned new tricks and made new friends—he stopped off in San Francisco. There he was impressed by magician H. P. Lovecraft at the Cannery, and the two men became friends immediately. Lovecraft encouraged him to come to San Francisco and offered him a place to stay. Butterfly was dubious at first, but only for a moment. He said, "Uh—gee, I don't know. I've got a house and all that back in Nashville—sure, I'll do it!" He tried out the streets of San Francisco and found them good, went back to Nashville and wound up his affairs, and moved to the West Coast. Within a year he had worked his way up to the prime time of Friday and Saturday nights at Pier 39.)

"This year has been like a dream come true for me, where I'm making a decent living doing what I want to do. I thought about that, and then I added a little bit at the very end of my show about doing what you want to do in this lifetime and being as free as you want to be—just have enough courage!"

Butterfly begins his act by involving the small children who cluster around him as he lays out his equipment. In a minute he has them lined up on one knee, each holding an unlit torch, scared but game as he warns them of the dangers of the fire he is about to produce. A crowd has gathered, and imperceptibly the show has begun. The torches are lit after several laugh-provoking false starts, and with falsetto cries of "Oo! Ouch! Ahg!" he juggles the fire in circles and loops and pinwheels of flame. "Now this is real fire, and to prove it—I'm going to burn this kid right here!" (Shrieks) "Ahh, I wouldn't really do that! I have the heart of a child. At home in a jar." His juggling is laced with bubbles of laughter that come not so much from funny lines as from his superb sense of timing, his voice that breaks unexpectedly into a treble squeak, and a sure control that lets the audience relax into the expectation of being amused. He flips on a tape recorder and juggles to the rich symphonic strains of the "William Tell Overture," in a visual parody of its pomposities and excesses. Then he tosses a club to five different people in the crowd, using each exchange to comedic effect: "That's a nice suit you have there, sir! Is it a Penyay?" (The man nods doubtfully) "Ah, a J. C. Penyay!" "Now, juggling is just throwing up and catching it, and I want to share that experience," he says, and asks them to toss him the clubs at the count of three. "I'm going to go right into a five-club juggle," he announces confidently. Of course, at the signal the throws go wildly astray, crashing and thumping around him while he cringes with arms over his head. Next, lunging into the crowd, he seizes a boy by the collar and drags him onto the stage, shouting triumphantly, "A volunteer!" He introduces him: "Ladies and gentlemen, I have here a trained child. His first trick is called 'lying down' "—and he whisks the boy off his feet and onto his back at center stage. "I am going to attempt to juggle these three 196-gram clubs over your body," he informs him. "Now this is for your enjoyment only." The child grins sheepishly, a tiny bit scared, but pleased with the attention. As Butterfly is whirling the clubs right over his victim's nose, he explains, "I did a lot of birthday parties when I was first starting out—now I'm getting back at these little suckers one by one!" In show after show the young volunteer, rather than being angry or embarrassed, became Butterfly's devoted fan and followed him about afterward with adoring eyes. Children seem undeterred by his sardonic jokes: "Never mind the children—there's plenty more where they came from!" or "Don't you wish birth control were retroactive?" Drunken hecklers are quickly demolished by his wit: "I hate alcoholics that don't stay anonymous" or "Achoo! Pardon me, I'm allergic to assholes!" For his finale, he brings out a unicycle and, using the two biggest men in the audience as helpers, elaborately establishes his incompetence at mounting the wiggling, lurching thing. Then with one bone-jarring bump, he is off the stage and hurling himself through the crowd on the single wheel, mouth wide open in a long howl of terror and dismay as he hurtles back and forth, around and behind, and up a ramp to the platform and a breathless safe landing.

The ending of his show is close to Butterfly's heart, and when he squeaks, "Now, this is sensitive, so—shut up, you creeps!" he means it. Balancing a long-stemmed red rose on his nose, he recites:

> It matters not
> The job you've got
> As long as you do it well.
> Things are made by plans well-laid;
> The test of time will tell.
> But how can you count
> Or know the amount
> Or the value of a man?
> By the show displayed,
> Or the beauty made
> By the touch of the juggler's hand.

And sweeping off his velvet cap, he bows from the waist with arms spread wide and the top of his head toward the audience to disclose the tattooed butterflies there that give him his name—and ensure that he will never return to the straight world.

The street makes strange colleagues, and a little juggler from Canada who calls himself Moishe is as different in background from Butterfly as is possible in the setting of North American society. Moishe is a waif, a street urchin, a gypsy. As a child he was shuffled about from foster home to foster home, and repeatedly ran away until, at the age of thirteen, he convinced the authorities that he could take care of himself. Now in his twenties, he has never known any other adult life but the streets. His flat Canadian voice contrasts oddly with his exotic appearance: An unkempt braid of long pale brown hair hangs almost to his waist, and a flat moustache stretches across his gentle elfin face to his earlobes. Scarves, beads, ribbons drip everywhere from his blousy shirt, embroidered vest, and patchwork pantaloons. Onstage he wears a top hat, which he balances on a cane on his chin to draw a crowd. Moishe is a competent if small-scale juggler. Several of his tricks are unusual: He controls three balls while rolling over onto his back; he includes a salt-shaker in an apple-and-ball juggle and salts the fruit in the air, and he bounces the balls in a cascade off his bent knee and foot. In his native country he traveled with the Caravan Stage Company, a group of thirty performers who went from town to town like medieval minstrels. They would arrive like a traditional circus, parading down the main street with a calliope, and during the day each individual performer would find a sidewalk corner for busking and hat-passing. At night they would join in a comedy musical indoors on a legitimate stage. Much to my astonishment, Moishe told me that there are a number of such traveling entertainment troupes in Canada, and they are government-sponsored. He himself is about to try for a Canadian performance grant to study advanced juggling; the requirements are two years of experience and a portfolio to prove it. "While you're on the grant you have to do a certain number of socially conscious gigs in hospitals and places like that," he explained, "but the government will set them up for you if you want."

Moishe, like nearly all jugglers, is self-taught. Observation, practice, and a book titled *Juggling Made Easy*, by Rudolf Dittrich, seem to be the three givens for mastering basic technique. There are very few classes in circus skills at colleges and universities. Hovey Burgess at New York University is outstanding. Some circuses have affiliated classes for hand-picked candidates, and mime schools, such as Carlo Manzzone-Clementi's Dell'arte School at Blue Lake, California, sometimes teach allied skills. Ed Jackman has taught Russian juggling at special classes at UCLA, and his partner, Daniel Rosen, learned at a juggling booth at the Los Angeles Renaissance Faire—and came back to be the teacher the next year.

Dave Finnigan, alias Professor Confidence, is attempting to fill that gap in learning opportunities for novice jugglers. He has formed a nationwide affiliation called the Juggling Institute that offers a full day of juggling instruction for elementary and secondary schools. The Professor has teaching teams active in Northern and Southern California, Texas, and the cities of Boston, Baltimore, Chicago, and Seattle. Their fee is usually paid by the PTA or student activity funds. For a modest amount they will come into a school, put on a performance to stir interest, and in gym classes teach every single student to do a cascade first with scarves, then bean bags, and finally real juggling balls. The Professor feels that mastering this skill gives a young person a great boost in confidence (thus his name).

He himself is a dedicated street performer (or "vaude-villian," as he calls it) and juggles on the street in any town to which his travels take him.

Jeff Chroman of San Diego's Balboa Park thinks of himself as a direct descendant and bearer of a far older tradition. His speech takes on an archaic rhythm as he describes his act: "I tell traditional juggling stories as they were taught to me by my grandfather, and before him his grandparents, and before them their grandparents in Albania." Jeff, who has just graduated in international relations at the University of California, was born in the United States but learned European juggling tales from his Albanian grandfather and his cronies. Jeff's eyes shine with devotion when he speaks of the old man. He was crippled by the time he was forty by a broken back and the hard work necessary to survive as an immigrant. Although he was unable to juggle for his grandson, he passed on the tradition in the form of the juggling stories that had held people spellbound in Albania for whole evenings at a time. Jeff's father was not interested in the old man's craft, and Jeff feels that most ethnic traditions in the United States have skipped a generation in this way. Although he is a superb juggler, he sees himself primarily as a storyteller, one who "plucks at words like people pluck at harps." Jeff's ambition is to rejuvenate the art of public storytelling, and he has used his background in international cultures to ferret out juggling stories from India, Africa, and the Orient. He is hopeful that the street will be the theater for reviving all kinds of other lost performance-arts.

At work on the sidewalk Jeff is a commanding figure in spite of his small size, sturdy with close-cropped dark brown hair and beard, slightly exotic in embroidered peasant shirt, corduroy knee pants, and knit socks. With deep professional zeal for excellence, he favors heavy, razor-sharp machetes and daggers and swords, although he is not above a comedy turn with "live" rubber fish. Although Jeff sees himself as part of the stream of tradition, he is not hidebound by it. He adapts freely for American audiences, and uses the old lines and stories as building blocks to create his own style. But when he launches into one of the old tales, and his audience stands rapt and involved, the shadowy presence of untold generations of street jugglers stretches behind him back into the beginnings of history.

———————————————— • ————————————————

JEFF CHROMAN TELLS AN ALBANIAN JUGGLING STORY

"I'm gonna tell you a legend amongst the jugglers. This legend said that when a juggler learns to love juggling more than he fears death he must go to the largest live volcano at the time, climb it, jump in, and while falling he must juggle three swords. If he can do that successfully he will not fall into the lava but will be miraculously saved.

"My own grandfather went on a pilgrimage—to Mount Vesuvius he went. And he climbed the mountain" (he mimes the action). "He climbed and he climbed and he climbed for days until he reached the summit, and there he peered in" (he staggers back with a small shriek). "My goodness, it was bubbling like hot chili! And it smelled a little like chili! But the moment had come, and the time to act, and my grandfather performed his predestined task and jumped into the crater of MOUNT VESUVIUS!

"Now, while falling through the mountain he whipped out these three swords and he began to juggle" (which he does) "and miraculously he was suspended in midair. Above his head he saw a white light he recognized—it was the juggling angel by the name of—Dora! And he greeted her in the traditional way. He says, 'How's your aura, Dora?' She just smiled. She says, 'Darlink, your juggling tasks shall now begin. Can you flip that little dagger in the air two times?' My grandfather says, 'No problem!' " (He does it) "She says, 'Can you throw that machete underneath your leg?' My grandfather says, 'It's gettin' touchy, but I think I can do it.' " (And he does) " 'And now for your last and final trick, darlink,' she says, 'can you take a slice out of the very air which you breathe?' My grandfather says, 'Is there anybody else up there I can talk to?' She says, 'Do it kid!' " (A mistake— he drops) "At that point my grandfather dropped the knife; Dora zoomed down and grabbed it. She handed it to my grandfather, winked her eye, and said, 'Don't worry about it, kid!' (Laughter and applause)

"For the last and final task, taking a slice out of the very air which he breathed in the middle of Mount Vesuvius—Yah! And once again—Yah! He did it! And once again—Yah! (Applause)

"Dora swooped down and grabbed my grandfather by the collar—his feet were dangling—and dragged him all the way out through Europe, dropped him in Albania, and kissed him right here on the forehead! Ladies and gentlemen, from that day forward if you looked at my grandfather when the sun was rising or when the sun was setting you could see shining right on his forehead like a diamond—the aura of Dora, the juggling angel!"

MAGICIANS

"Observe that at no time do the fingers leave the hand."
—Traditional

"Magic is one of the most frightening things in the performing arts, because if you blow it, it's blown for good. You can't save your act," said circus entrepreneur Nick Weber. A juggler who drops can pick up the moment with a fast quip and a quick grab; a tightrope artist who falls can climb back up on the wire; a musician who makes a mistake can sing louder. But a magician who errs is exposed and undone. "People like to be fooled, but they don't like to be made fools of," as H. P. Lovecraft pointed out. So magic on the street, in broad daylight with spectators watching close from front, sides, and back, is risky.

In spite of the difficulties, magic has always existed in its purest form on the streets, says Harry Anderson. From shamans to witch doctors to fakirs and fire walkers, magic has always found a ready public in the village and the marketplace. The Hindu rope trick may be explainable, but we really don't want it explained away. We want to believe with just a tiny corner of our mind that it could be real. On the stage, with crafty lighting and mirrors and curtains, no matter how elaborate the illusion we are puzzled but not truly convinced. On television there is no belief at all—we know that the director can make anything happen by cutting the film. But on the street, eyeball to eyeball and under the sun, there a conjuror can be truly magical. "How did he do that!" we cry involuntarily. We saw it, and then we didn't. We know that can't be, but yet—

"What we consider to be common sense is nothing more than a collection of prejudices gathered before the age of sixteen," said Harry Lovecraft as we sat talking late one night in a San Francisco café. We had been speaking of Uri Geller and his ability to bend spoons with his mind. Harry had taken up two matching spoons, and now he was rubbing one with his forefinger and concentrating on its shiny surface. "Magic is a visual Zen koan, a visual riddle," he intoned. Then he laid the spoon next to its mate and—they no longer matched! One bent away at an oblique angle. For a second I was amazed, but then his wife Patty laughed. "Harry, not again! You'll get us thrown out of every café in town!" and I realized that he had bent the second spoon in his lap while I gazed at the first. An object lesson in the art of patter, the deliberate distraction of attention.

Lovecraft, who has worked the Cannery stage since 1972, is an extraordinary magician, a man devoted to magic since his early childhood. He was trained by retired vaudevillians "here in San Francisco at the old Golden Gate Magic Company. When I was a little kid I used to come up here on the bus with my twenty or thirty bucks that I'd earned mowing lawns and throwing newspapers.

Tom, the guy that owned the shop, would run around all day long showing me everything in the store. I'd be there when he opened the door in the morning, and I wouldn't go home until they locked the door at night. I'd go up there on Saturdays because that was the day the old cronies would come out and sit around the shop and swap stories. As an exercise they used me as their receptacle to pour all of the incredible knowledge that they had from a lifetime of experience in show business. They had no one else to pass all this information, this knowledge, on to. It was not considered to be of value because it was an age that was past. But I was interested; I would buy the tricks that I wanted, and they would teach them to me. They had a little stage there they would put me up on, and then they would have a committee and they'd teach me everything, how to do it. If I'd make a mistake they'd say 'NO, no, no, this is why . . . Always keep . . . This is how . . .' It was very regimented and disciplined, but I just ate it up. So all of them would devote the entire day to teaching me theater, vaudeville." As he grew up, Harry had a brief fling with the straight world as a manager of a J. C. Penney's department store. "It was a boring trap," he frowned. "The boss was a jerk—I was just not a company man." Preferring to be his own boss, he sold washing machines while studying theater.

Harry puts his dramatic training to good use in his act. Most magicians develop a stage persona, and Harry's is the archetypical American medicine man—the brash, fast, and fancy-talking huckster. In a nasal voice dripping with unctuous deceit, he says, "Looky, looky, looky, I've got it here and I'm gonna show it to you now—the most phantasmagorical congregation of wondrous novelties, cosmic mysteries, and legerdemain ever to transvert the byways of America." He lights two torches, and throwing back his head, lowers the fire slowly down his throat. "Tongue flambé!" he announces, and this time when he withdraws the torches little flames flicker eerily from the end of his tongue. He takes the fire on his fingertips and flicks it away, and then reels yards and yards of colored tape from his mouth. A live dove flutters suddenly in his grasp ("My assistant, Eggbert") to demonstrate the curative qualities of Dr. Lovecraft's Wonder Elixir ("a polydramatic panacea"). "My friends, if you can hardly get to bed at night, and then if you can hardly get it up—out of bed in the morning, if whether you get up or don't, your get up and go has got up and went, and you got that dark brown taste in your mouth and you hurt all over worse than the other places—well, my friends, you've come to the right spot, because I have here the greatest manufactured product since the wheel." Eggbert, he declaims, before the application of the Wonder Cure Elixir, "was so weak that he could not walk or fly and had not a single pinfeather to his scrawny little body. He was for all practical intents and purposes at death's door. (*At death's door*, dummy!)" he hisses at the bird, who rolls over and lies stiff, claws pointing skyward. "But now—do a little yoga for them here, Eggbert. Show 'em how you stand on your head!" And he does—with some coaxing—on Harry's palm. "I say the magic words—'Colonel Sanders'—and there we are!" He pops the bird into a paper bag, crumples it up, reaches in and pulls out an egg, and throws away the empty bag. The egg is then broken into a pan, bursts into flame, and when the pan is uncovered, there are some very real peanut butter cookies, which he passes out to the children. All the time his mile-a-minute mouth goes on in authentic style, a blend between W. C. Fields and the Wizard of Oz.

Although he does get around later in his act to the more traditional linking rings and card tricks, Harry is more imaginative and flamboyant in his effects than most street magicians. Partly this is because he is a very superior showman, but also it is because on the Cannery stage he has the advantages of darkness and a seated audience. Magicians who work right out on the daylit sidewalk are limited to those tricks that are angle-proof, need no resetting, and are easily transportable. These requirements translate into six types of tricks: the linking rings, the disappearing sponge balls, the cut-and-restored rope and the Professor's Nightmare, scarf or coin vanishes, and card tricks done with oversize pasteboards for easy visibility. This rather limited repertoire depends on clever patter and smooth sleight-of-hand for effectiveness, and all of the necessary equipment can be packed into a case or backpack or small suitcase.

R. J. Lewis of New York is impressively organized on the street. Costumed in well-tailored black pants and vest and black turtleneck, he arrives at his street corner carrying a slim and elegant briefcase. When opened, it reveals compartments for rope, balls, coins, a holder for the rings and the tip can, and a set of folding metal legs that convert the closed case into a little table. His specialty is coin tricks, and he takes pride in the skill of his vanishes and color transformations with quarters. Tall and svelte and trimly bearded, R. J. is scrupulous about his appearance. "This is the same outfit I wear at the Playboy Club," he said. "A street performer should always dress nice. The better you dress the more money you make. If you dress like a bum, you make money like a bum. If you dress like a professional, you make money like a professional." R. J. has been on the street four years and usually performs on Shubert Alley just off Times Square at theater time. He makes a living at it during the warm months, and in the winter he depends on private parties and nightclubs, and his other career—acting.

LOOKING FOR THE LOOKOUT

Up ahead through the streams of people on Fifth Avenue we see a knot of spectators draw around a handsome young black man. A street performer? I stroll up; from the edge of the circle I see his gesticulating hands over a pasteboard box, the cards laid out—a magician? There is money on the box, lots of it. Tens, twenties—the man is talking, moving the cards, and a groan goes up from the crowd. More money is handed over . . . It is a magician, in the ancient sense. This is three-card monte, a version of the old, old shell game, and it is strictly illegal and completely ubiquitous in New York. We walk on hurriedly, and there on the next corner we see the lookout lounging against a building with sharp eyes alert for the police. "When the cops come by, the lookout whistles, the cardsharp kicks over the box, pockets the money, and walks away," I had been told. Soon it becomes a game to spot the confederate whenever we see the game. In Central Park on a bench, on Sixth Avenue waiting to cross the light but never leaving the curb, on Madison pretending to gaze in a shop window. Even Alice and I, in our West Coast naïveté, can finger them every time. Later I ask a real magician about the odds. "There's no way to win," he declares flatly. "It's done with sleight; it's a clip game. But it's probably been a popular street hustle throughout eternity."

Dean of New York street magicians is Jeff Sheridan, who has been a busker almost as long as violinist Richard Wexler. Indeed, he began his career as a sidewalk prestidigitator by doing card tricks after Richard's show. Nowadays Jeff's spot is at the foot of the Sir Walter Scott statue in Central Park Mall. He has written a book on the history of the art, titled *Street Magic*.

Another New York magician is David Strassman, a tri-vocational performer who is clear about his priorities: "I'm an actor, who's a ventriloquist, who does magic." David is a silent conjuror; although he doesn't wear the classical whiteface, he mimes his reactions and expectations during the magic act, and whistles like Harpo Marx to get attention and signal the changes. He finds this freedom from dependency on language is useful in Europe and in noisy street environments. Some ability at mime is perhaps essential for a magician; as Boston juggler-magician Dario demonstrated, "Nothing ever really disappears unless you pretend and believe in it yourself." He gestured and an imaginary something was there—and then gone. "You can see it without my having anything at all in my hand."

Like most of his colleagues, David Strassman does the vanishing foam rubber balls—he hands one to a volunteer, and a moment later when the clenched fist is opened there are two—and rope tricks. The cut-and-restored rope is a common street effect. Its allied illusion, the oddly named Professor's Nightmare, uses three pieces of rope—a short, medium, and long—that repeatedly become the same length, or even one long piece. But David's best moment comes when he borrows an expensive jacket from a spectator and grinds a burning cigarette down into the fabric wadded in his fist. Peering down into the smoking hole, he whistles with horror for a suspenseful moment, and then shakes the jacket out to show it unharmed.

The Slidoni toilet-paper deception, a favorite of messy juggler Mike Davis, is another trick that shows up often on the street. A volunteer is invited into the circle ("Stand right over here on the trapdoor, sir!") and is seated on a box and told to lean forward and hold a roll of toilet paper on two outstretched forefingers. Then the magician, with appropriate patter, tears off a few squares, crumples them up, and working close to the volunteer's face, flicks the wad over his head in a sleight-of-hand pass. To the victim it seems as if the paper has miraculously vanished, but the audience is gleefully aware of the deceit. The trick is good for several repetitions before the magician finally takes mercy and has the volunteer turn his head to see the crumpled evidence of his own gullibility strewn behind him.

The Slidoni trick sometimes tempts the magician to X-rated patter, which can be a problem on the street where every show is a family show, at least in the daytime. Illusions that are too bloody can also be too strong for the street. Jonathan Szeles of San Francisco had to abandon his best trick after some parents wrote letters complaining to the management of Pier 39. They were afraid their children would try to emulate Jonathan's spectacular theatrics: He would eat a number of razor blades, swallow yards of thread and then retrieve it with the blades strung along its length, accompanied by gushes of stage blood from a bladder hidden under his tongue. Jonathan, like many street magicians and jugglers, is also a skilled fire-eater. The secret, he divulged, is to breathe out as the fire goes in, so a layer of air protects the skin. But if the weather is windy, as it often is in San Francisco, the fire is apt to blow to the unprotected sides of the lip. He learned the vagaries of fire the hard way; in a trick he has now abandoned, he would take a gulp of gasoline and spit it out in a stream at a lighted candle. A huge flame would billow up and the audience would applaud wildly—until the time when the fluid spilled down his neck and chin, ignited, and wouldn't go out no matter how much he beat at it. "Blisters on your face are very detrimental to your act," he said ruefully.

Jonathan's more conventional tricks are nicely linked

with glib and amusing patter; he prefers to think of himself as a comedian. He began performing magic at seventeen, and is now only twenty, although his stage image—a wicked and slightly addled professor in rusty frock coat and wire-rimmed glasses—seems much older. He sees the street as an important stepping-stone in his career; it has led to clubs and other indoor work for him, and now he has ambitions toward television—the Merv Griffin show, or perhaps *Make Me Laugh*. "If I hadn't gone on the street, I'd probably be working at McDonald's someplace now," he levels. Many of his best lines have come from hecklers; in doing eight shows a day he estimates that he picks up at least three new lines. For instance, once while he was eating razor blades, a drunk yelled out, "That must taste like Schick!" Jonathan immediately incorporated it into his nightclub routine.

"Since you're such a marvelous crowd, I'm going to kill myself for you," announces Peter Sosna of Boston, tying a rope snugly around his neck. He persuades a boy in the audience to give the dangling end a sharp tug, and the noose comes away intact, apparently passing through his throat whole. Such minor shockers are only the warm-up for what is perhaps the most elaborate magic act on the street, using a small truckload of equipment and a variety of effects never attempted by other outdoor magicians. In typical Bostonian style Peter began small four years ago ("I'd go up to groups of people on the street with my briefcase and accost them: 'Here, let me show you some magic!' "), and as he made money he bought more and more equipment and expanded his act in the welcoming atmosphere of Harvard Square. Today he can do two completely different twenty-five-minute shows. He cuts a person in half with a buzzing chainsaw ("I'll just tuck this cloth around you—the last person we did this to bled like a pig!"), slides out the midsection of his pretty assistant

Gene Judd links rings in Philadelphia

as she stands smiling out of a big upright box, and ends
the act with a spectacular trunk-vanish: After the assistant has been bagged and locked in a trunk, he stands on
top and in a twinkling she appears in his place, while he, a
moment later, is discovered in the bag, in the trunk—and

wearing different clothes. "How do you do such tricks right out on the street?" I marveled. "Are they angle-proof?"

"Well—ah—almost," he confessed.

Like most magicians Peter has been entranced with the conjuror's art since he was a small child, and now, with his repertoire and his tools perfected on the street, he is beginning to be widely in demand at clubs and parties.

Most street magicians have indoor ambitions, but black Philadelphia conjuror Gene Judd is unusual in that he has recently come to the sidewalk from a flourishing ten-year career in stage magic. During the Bicentennial in the City of Brotherly Love, entertainers were encouraged in the streets, and since that time a number of buskers have flourished there. Gene finds that he can make enough in a good summer on Chestnut Street to live all the rest of the year. He still continues to do banquets, parties, and trade shows, though, and finds the visibility on the street a help to getting bookings. This is true for most street performers. All prestidigitators, however, hate children's birthday parties. "It's easier to fool a college professor than a small child," said Lovecraft. "They'll catch you every time. They live in a world of magic; it doesn't mean a damn thing to them. They just want to get into the show and play with your toys."

———————————————————•———————————————————

HARRY ANDERSON DABBLES IN GORE

A unicorn skull sits on a lace doily on the TV table in the Hollywood apartment of Leslie and Harry Anderson. Three magicians are lolling on the couch talking shop, and I am curled up in an armchair hoping they have forgotten that I am listening. They argue comparative merits of cotton vs. nylon rope for the Professor's Nightmare, the illusions of Uri Geller ("They have him investigated by all kinds of committees from universities, but you notice they never send a team of magicians to check him out . . ."), tricks that went wrong ("I flipped the cigarette and instead of going up my sleeve it dropped in my pocket, and damned if two minutes later smoke didn't start pouring out of my pants like a Chaplin movie . . .").

Harry is reminded of a story from his days on the street. At that time he sometimes worked movie queues, and like all savvy performers he tried to match the flavor of his show to the theme of the movie. On this particular occasion the film was *Jaws*. "I got one of those thin loaves of French bread, and I ran a rubber tube up the center of it. Then I filled the tube with stage blood, and soaked the whole thing; I put it up my sleeve, and fastened on an artificial hand." After doing a few opening tricks to disarm the audience, he reached under his table, pulled out a meat cleaver, and whacked off the hand. "Oh, it made a lovely sound!" he gloated. "The stump just lay there pulsing gore." After one paralyzed moment of shocked horror, the audience rose up in wrath and came at him. "I thought they were going to kill me! I grabbed my stuff and ran for my life—I'm telling you, I never did that trick again. If any of you guys want some French bread, I've got a lot of it left over!"

The triumvirate of street magicians in the United States is H. P. Lovecraft, Jeff Sheridan, and Harry Anderson. They were the pioneers, the first on the street, and of the three only Harry Anderson is no longer working outdoors. The beginnings of modern street performing and the beginnings of Harry Anderson's career as a conjuror coincided. He was one of the first buskers in San Francisco in 1968, when he was sixteen. During his high school and college years he worked seasonally at the Cannery, and later, after an acting stint with the Oregon Shakespeare Festival, became the very first street performer in Austin, Texas ("except for a guy who sold coffins on the sidewalk," he qualifies). For a time he worked college campuses, setting up a tent and doing a forty-five-minute show, and then in 1976 he was lured to New Orleans by the Mardi Gras. "I spent two nights in jail, but I made a fortune," he reminisced. Two months later he moved there, just in time for the year-long moratorium on street performing resulting from Scotty Hill's arrest. Harry managed to get hired by the city recreational department to do magic shows in housing projects, and also worked for a coalition of merchants, the French Market Guild. Together with one-man band Professor Gizmo he initiated a lawsuit against the city to attempt to lift the ban, but soon concluded that New Orleans was "not a good city to cause a ruckus in unless you know people." He returned to San Francisco and the Cannery, and after some time there on the street he began to focus more on college tours and nightclub work, married mentalist Leslie, and joined talents with her in an act that now is a headline attraction in Las Vegas and Tahoe, in clubs, and on television. "But the street was certainly where I learned how to do magic, and where I learned to love magic."

In a nostalgic mood, Harry remembered the flavor of his street days in San Francisco. "My whole life was at the Cannery. My girl friend worked at the Cannery, and I ate at the Cannery, and I hung out at the bookstore, and it was just like the office—being at the Cannery. I'd go sometimes at eight o'clock in the morning to get a spot on Bay Street and sit around till ten, and then do some warm-up shows just for the street rats, folks hanging out, you know, and then I'd work all day and usually quit around four thirty, doing maybe eight shows."

Harry spoke of the energy drain on the street that never allowed him the freedom to create new material. "You're a magician second; you're a street performer first. You watch other street performers; you live and breathe street performing. I was so exhausted by the end of the day that I would never pick up a magic book or a trick to learn. I experimented some on the street, but it was my livelihood, and I had to make sure I was going to make money. I think street performers feel more pressure than cabaret performers, because there's a certain scrounging quality about being on the street that keeps you going. You have to keep pulling yourself along. Even when you're making good money there's still that feeling of dragging it out of them. It's a challenge—and that makes for pressure."

In struggling with the eternal street problem of holding an audience's attention, Harry hit on a principle he later came to call the "drag-out." "My theory—and it worked— was to start something, get them involved, and then they have to stay to see it end." For instance, he would borrow a dollar bill and burn it, and then, a long time later, it would appear in what seemed to be another trick. "The end of a trick is a climax, a finish point, and a person could very naturally get up and leave at that point. So I started just wiring little things together but keeping a long string of suspense all the way through. I would have a girl choose a card, and fifteen minutes later, after I'd shot her with a toy gun and blindfolded myself and gone through a lot of hysterics, the card would end up in a sealed envelope." The drag-out principle can be seen in the most dynamic street-magic acts.

Harry's stage persona, he says, is "coarse, insulting, absurd, offbeat," almost the antithesis of his real character. In creating this image he discovered that "it wasn't the magic I was selling—I was selling myself. I was using magic to create a situation, and I was playing with the situation. I had a woman on stage choose a card, and the first time I didn't give her a chance to look at it, and the second time she wouldn't get a chance to put it back in the deck, and I'm responsible but I'm blaming her for screwing up the trick all along the way, and I'm getting hostile. Finally I pull out a gun . . . You see, I'm creating a situation on stage that is theater, and I use the magic as a reason for coming out on stage, and for getting off stage, but the part in between is playing with the character."

In the hands of a worker of only minor miracles, this groping toward a dramatic persona can take the imitative form of elaborate period costuming. Jerry Salazar, a former San Francisco coffeehouse close-up magician ("a table-hopper"), looks as if he has stepped directly out of 1929: knickers and close-fitting corduroy jacket, saddle shoes and argyle socks, a bow tie and cap. But in the hands of an instinctive showman a character can be central to a coherent magic act, because the essence of theater is the impact of a personality on an audience.

Magical Mystical Michael has developed one of the most memorable street characters. An itinerant magician who lives out of a well-outfitted van, he is liable to turn up almost anyplace, and once seen, his colorful figure is hard to forget. Over a full-sleeved purple shirt and bloused Turkish pants of a faded russet color, he wears a blue vest embroidered on the back with a big red rose, and dozens of tasseled pouches and purses of velvet and leather hang from his waist. His cheerful, wide-mouthed face and rosy cheeks are framed by a short golden beard in which are braided a whole orchestra of little tinkling bells. When a

Jerry Salazar shuffles the cards on the streets of San Francisco

trick succeeds, he scrunches down his neck coyly, tilts his head, and giggles a high-pitched, manic "Hee, hee, hee!" As this street character evolved, he found that some of his tricks didn't fit, and so he uses another image indoors for the leftovers—Wonderful Waldo, a rumpled elderly wizard. "Once you get a character," he explained, "then you got something to work with. Instead of working on your magic, you can work on your *act*."

Magical Mystical Michael—born Michael Kaufman—was seduced by magic five years ago while he was studying at the University of Colorado at Boulder. One day he saw a magician on campus who did a trick with a sword that changed colors. "It baffled my head. So I was walking down the street and there was a magic shop there; I walked in and asked the guy about the trick and he sold it to me. It was $2.50. I went home and I practiced about four days and I couldn't figure it out—it wouldn't work right. So I went back to him and he showed me how to do it. Then I was really into it. I was working as a busboy at the college, and during my breaks I'd go out on the patio and take a break and do this magic trick for a few people and they'd go '*Wow!*' " Michael was entranced by the reaction. He kept going back to the shop for more tricks, and searching for new audiences. "You start with who you're living with; they get sick of it pretty quick—'Aw no, not another one, Michael!'—and then you go to friends' parties and do a little magic set, you know. They dig it, so there's another party coming up in about two weeks, so you go home and learn some more new tricks. After a while you get like a twenty-minute little routine." From there he progressed to benefits, open mikes, and finally got permission to perform and pass the hat at a club while the band took a break. By this time his magic was paying the rent, so when the Boulder Mall opened in 1977 he was one of the first performers to take advantage of it. There he found that street technique was an art. "I couldn't hold a crowd," he lamented. It took a while for him to learn the basics. "People aren't in the streets to see your show— they're in the streets to see everything. So you gotta stop 'em. And then you gotta keep 'em there. And then you have to keep 'em long enough to get finished with your show, and you gotta make sure they like it enough so when you pass the hat you make a livin'." By August of that year he had his act together. He bought a van and set out for a two-month vacation—and has been on the road ever since. "I like traveling because of the changes," he says. "It makes me be me." Like most itinerants he performs often on college campuses and at Renaissance Faires. At first he had problems learning to speak the Elizabethan dialect required by most Faire managements: "It was worse than learning Hebrew for my bar mitzvah," he revealed. Michael's middle-class Jewish parents were uneasy about his chosen vocation, but when they saw him perform at his sister's wedding last year they became reconciled to his way of life.

It is hard not to be impressed with Michael's mental and physical health—he blooms with happy good sense and good living. He eats a simple pure diet of fruits and vegetables, grains, and nuts ("I grow sprouts in my van") and does yoga for one or two hours every morning. "My goal in life is to be as enlightened as I can and as healthy as I can," says he. "I don't work on my show—I work on my life!"

In performance Michael shows a sure control of the audience. He draws a crowd with a weird noisemaker he calls a flexitone—a metal tongue that vibrates against a handle to produce a loud dinging, fluctuating tone up and down the scale. When he has a circle of curious onlookers, he says, "You're probably saying to yourselves right now, 'Who is this guy and what does he do?' Let me show you a little bit of my magic credentials, which you'll probably want to see before the show actually starts. I got here a silk handkerchief. What I'm gonna do is I'm gonna poke it down in the palm of my hand and before your eyes it's gonna vanish. I'm gonna tell you what I'm doing because when I do it and it's done you're not gonna be confused about what happened! Hee, hee, hee! Pouf! Pouf! And red isn't even my favorite flavor!" Now, having gained the attention of fifty or sixty people, he announces that the show will last fifteen minutes, and invites those who want to stay to come up to the front row and sit down, thus allowing people to establish the intention of remaining. His repertoire includes the usual sponge balls, ropes, cards, and the linking rings—at which he is a master. He uses eight (three or six is standard), and after he has exhausted the possibilities of amazement from the rings passing through each other and linking in midair, he goes on to do an encyclopedia of elaborate sculptures with them. But his best effect, and a trick that is also used as a drag-out by Jonathan in San Francisco, starts with an orange. "The world's smallest pumpkin!" he announces, and entrusts it to a male volunteer to hold aloft. "Get it up, there!" he cries at intervals thereafter. Another volunteer, usually a pretty girl, chooses a card and is encouraged to tear it into pieces, which vanish from Michael's hands—all except one fragment, which he gives back to her to keep. At last, with great drama, the orange is sliced open, and there inside is a folded card, the same number and suit as the one that was demolished. There is, however, just one corner missing, which exactly fits the piece the volunteer is holding.

I watched Michael demonstrate his crowd control at the Mardi Gras under three circumstances that would have undone a lesser busker. In the middle of his orange trick an ambulance drowned him out with screaming sirens. He reached into his pack and shot it with a water pistol; the audience laughed and applauded and waited until he could go on. Later, during another performance, a parade turned the corner and headed straight for the space where he was in midshow. Without missing a beat he quickly wound up the trick and asked for half a tip because they had seen only half a show. A third time a jazz band with tap dancers struck up not twenty-five feet from where he was just beginning his last trick. He was unflustered, and even slowed his delivery just a bit while he held the audience's attention by sheer willpower to the end.

But the busker with a really astonishing ability at crowd control is Will the Juggler. Although he tosses torches and swords, he considers himself a magician "because I'm dealing with that kind of energy. To me the real trick, the magic, is to start out with a bunch of people walking along with their hands in their pockets and long faces and end up with a crowd of people having fun together, smiling and clapping." And this is exactly what he does. He doesn't so much perform as orchestrate an audience. Will is a true star, like Peter Damien and Butterfly and Richard Wexler, and his enchantment is powerful. He never has to work at drawing a crowd; he steps out into the space, does a few warm-up exercises, and there are a hundred people waiting quietly to see what happens next. He might be a pirate, with his long curly black hair drawn back with a scarf and one gold earring setting off his swarthy complexion. Or, in tunic and sash, he is a reincarnation of the medieval jongleur. The impression is intensified when he blows a conch shell to attract even more people, the primeval sound echoing from the surrounding buildings. Fast patter and snappy lines are not for Will; with simple earnestness he explains, "We're going to make some magic here right out in front of you—no hocus-pocus. Anybody can make magic—you don't need to be a magician. Three things you *do* need: Faith—you gotta believe in yourself and you can do anything. Rhythm—get in tune with what you're do-

Will pierces a balloon with a knitting needle—and concentration

ing. And concentration—pulling it all together and bringing it down to a pinpoint. We're going to try one of each of those." Faith and rhythm he produces with balances and juggles with knives, torches, and fire sticks, while the crowd accompanies him in a steady, intense clapping. Soon a tangible group-cohesion begins to develop, a community identity among these people who had been assorted pedestrians a moment before. Will is almost mystical about this phenomenon—he is convinced that group consciousness is the necessary prelude to universal consciousness. He also feels a responsibility to educate people about street theater, and when he has focused their attention and drawn a laugh with a fake sword-swallow, he says a few words about street performing and thanks New Orleans for being one of the few cities that allow it. Before his finale, he announces, "I still see some people in the back row looking glum. Up to now the show has been free, but the price of admission from here on is a smile." Inviting people to come forward, to sit down close, he produces a balloon, inflates it, and proposes to pierce it with a long spike without bursting it. "We can all do this together," he says. "Take a deep breath and concentrate on the outside shape of the balloon. Don't let it disappear." Then he slowly, slowly inserts the spike—all the way—and then slowly, slowly withdraws it, while a crowd of hundreds stands utterly silent and completely focused on the tiny movement in his hands, convinced they are taking part in the magic. The spike is safely out; the balloon is intact; he jabs it with the point, and the sharp pop releases the crowd into cheers and applause. "Now!" he says. "You wanta see me do something *really* dangerous?" He drags out a bundle in a blanket, throws open the four corners, and reveals a heap of wicked, jagged broken pieces of beer bottles, jars, glasses. "I'm gonna walk across this in my bare feet," he announces. "But you gotta help me." He takes off his shoes and steps out carefully across the vicious points and glittering edges, sustained by the concentration and faith of the group he has created—the true magic.

MIMES AND CLOWNS

"**************? *****************!!"

—Traditional

Mime is the easiest pitch to do badly on the street, and the hardest to do well. Anybody with a tube of white grease-paint can get out there and pretend to know what they're doing, and many do. "It's easier than pushing drugs," grinned a middle-aged San Francisco busker, and he was only half-joking. "I was hungry; I came down here to the Wharf when I first got into town, and I saw this guy miming. I said, 'I could do that!' " Another mime showed him where to buy the makeup and how to apply it, and he went out and made a living with a shuffle-walk and a single pose. Eg Mahan has built a career on the streets of West-wood Village from one gimmick—a thirty-second mock wedding. A common sight on Jefferson Street in Fisher-man's Wharf—"Mime Alley"—are young black children decked out in whiteface, curly gray wig, pipe, and derby who perform a stiff, jerky robot-mime to disco music from a transistor radio. Like all children, they are cute, but talent and training are completely lacking, and their antics are merely appealing hypes.

It is evidence of the power of the mime that such amateurish attempts are tolerated on the street. A juggler or a magician displaying an equal degree of incompetence would be ignored and left penniless. But the deathly figure of the mime, the clown, the fool, resonates in our collective unconscious with terror as well as laughter. On the street the imaginary fourth wall that shields us from the performer is fragile. We gather around to be amused, but we are also afraid—from this comes the fascination. Even the clumsiest of mimes recognizes this attraction/repulsion and uses it by interacting with the audience. They imitate passersby; they create imaginary objects and hand them to spectators; they set up little dramas and involve observers. Watch the faces of a street mime's audience: They laugh and smile, but uncertainly—wanting to be approached and touched with that power, but dreading it, too.

In the history of clowning, mime has been a recurring theme, an art that emerged for both political and practical reasons, then faded and was reborn in another era. John H. Towsen traces its evolution in his excellent study, *Clowns*. The so-called mimes of ancient Greece were not silent, but the earliest form of clown theater. The Roman pantomime was closer to our concept of the art: "a solo dancer silently portraying all the characters (*panto* = all) in a story narrated by a chorus." In the Middle Ages itinerant street clowns continued to be called mimes until the ninth century, when the word jongleur came into fashion. From the Italian commedia dell'arte of the sixteenth to the eighteenth centuries emerged the character Pierrot, who developed into our modern mime. Pierrot, the only member of the commedia cast to whiten his face, was adapted by the great Jean-Gaspard Debureau when, in both England and France during the eighteenth century, popular nonaristocratic entertainment was subject to frequent political harassment. The fairground actors resorted to all sorts of trickery to get around the restrictions. Silence was one of their stratagems. In England the resulting dramatic form evolved for a time into the elaborate pantomimes, which only later resumed the use of dialogue. In France the restrictions caused the art of silent acting to flourish in Debureau's Théâtre des Funambules, a golden age that has been made famous by Marcel Carné's film *Children of Paradise.* In the twentieth century the electronic limitations of the early motion pictures resulted in another golden age of mime in the silent films of Chaplin and Keaton—and, later, in the different silence of Harpo Marx. Not until the late 1920s did modern mime appear, in Paris in the workshops of Jacques Copeau, which influenced the four great French mimes Etienne Decroux, Jean-Louis Barrault, Jacques Lecoq, and Marcel Marceau. Their performances and teaching have inspired hundreds of disciples throughout the world who have brought the art to heights of skill and subtlety. "In another ten years America will have a great mime age," said Marcel Marceau. "Mime is so old and so young. The danger is wanting to grow too fast without matching technique with depth, without learning to dwell in the silence, to swim in the musicality of the movements."

To match technique with depth the great street mime must be in touch with his or her own psyche and be willing to project that understanding in complete spontaneity and interaction with the moment and circumstances. The juggler is motivated by control—control of objects in defiance of gravity. The magician too works for control—of the beliefs and expectations of the audience. Only the mime must give up control and let the moment happen. A juggler or magician can rehearse and perfect an act by repetition, but a mime has only the security of technique and a vocabulary of set bits with which to create anew at every performance. Add to this the basic street difficulties of drawing a crowd, holding their interest, and building to a point of completion for passing the hat, and it becomes clear why so many sidewalk mimes settle for the safety of poses and small, predictable interchanges.

Ira Turner learned from books and has been a mime for five years. He is pragmatic about his craft: "I'm basically a street performer who studied on my own to learn how to do what I'm doing in order to pay my rent." He follows the tourists, staying in San Francisco from spring until the end of October, and then moving to New Orleans for the winter and Mardi Gras. In his top hat and tailcoat with purple velvet lapels, Ira is a mechanical grotesque. He hunches his shoulders (he can dislocate them at will) and skims along the ground in a humpbacked walk with his arms swinging rigidly at his sides. "I scare little kids to death," he admits. As a robot masher he pursues a hapless pretty girl from the audience, reaching stiffly out with clawed hands, his eyebrows wagging up and down in eternally unfulfilled lust. One of his best bits is a William Tell sketch: He establishes a round, red apple (taking a juicy bite), and then sets it carefully on the head of a woman. He backs off, takes aim with his bow, fires an arrow. Horrors! He has missed. He covers his eyes, peeks, then retrieves the shaft from the chest of another spectator, and finishes off the apple.

A self-styled loner, Ira is naturally armored and insulated, and so feels no need to hide behind the mask of whiteface. Sometimes he doesn't even bother with it: "I've come out here without the face on, and I made my money." He uses waterbase white rather than the more usual clown

Ira checks the shaft of an arrow

white, a makeup that is less masklike and more transparent but easily sweats off on hot days. With his face on he has no problem drawing a crowd. "It's a horror, actually. Because I can stop sometimes just to light a cigarette and all these people will start gathering around me."

The intense concentration in performance can be a mental drain, he says: "It sort of stupefies you if you do it too long." He has had short memory-lapses from extended mime sessions, and now limits himself to an hour. The freeze can be a rest period in mid-performance. Ira describes the mental process of putting himself in a trance-like pose: "I'll look at something that's across the street, and I'll concentrate on it. Say it's a corner of a building; I'll say to myself, 'Look, there's lines and they're all going into one point, even my line of sight is going into that one point. I'm just becoming part of that stationary one point; I'm not moving any more than it is.'"

His years on the street have taught him more and more about meeting the demands of an audience, and the evidence of his growing skill is the ever-increasing crowds he attracts. But sometimes he gets depressed because he still is not making what he feels he is worth, and he chafes at the life-style limitations of his small income. "I've made over a thousand dollars since I got here two months ago," he said, woefully, in New Orleans, "but I'm still sleeping in my car because nearly all of that went for engine repairs."

GUSTAVO STAYS SILENT

Gustavo is eating his lunch, sitting on the curb around a planter, his brown paper bag beside him. A little way

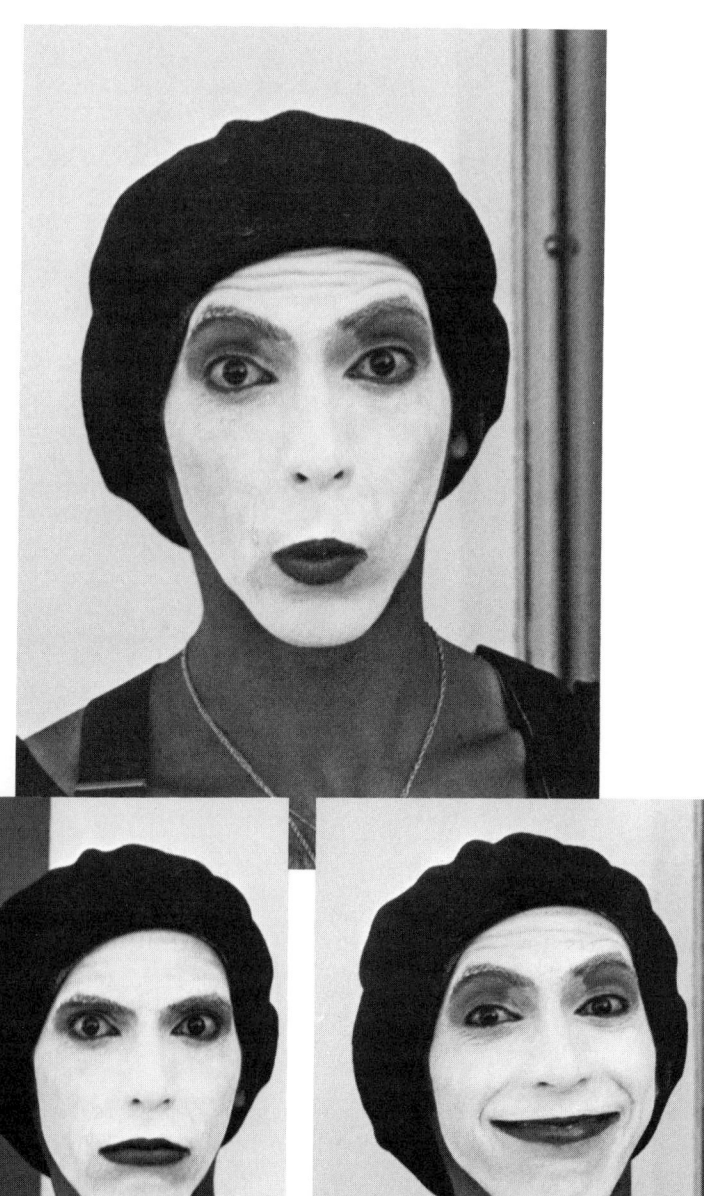

Gustavo's face

off, the tourists stream past clutching hot dogs and balloons and ignoring the bony mime in the beret as he hunches over his sandwich. All week I have been wanting to talk to him as I watched his strange grimaces and Chaplin walk, but I am hesitant to break through the mute illusion that surrounds a mime. But now I have found him in a semiprivate moment, so I squat down next to him, introduce myself, ask if we can talk. He gazes at me with questioning eyes and I see that up close his face is even stranger; nothing human shows through the heavy white paint, the black, black eyes. He gestures—a slow graceful circling of the hand that indicates the whole of his masked face. Then he lays one finger on his lips and moves his head from side to side in negation.

"You don't like to talk in makeup?" I ask. "Then how can I find out about you?"

He lifts one hand with the thumb and little finger extended outward, the other fingers folded against his palm. He lays the thumb against his ear; the little finger touches his lips. A telephone. "Shall I call you, then?" He nods, gives me his card, and his pale face moves in a slow, wide, carmine-lipped smile. "The Joker!" I think, and a chill that has nothing to do with the sea breeze touches the back of my neck.

The isolation of body parts that is characteristic of some American mime can result in deliberately robot-like mime characters. Andre Harvey, a strikingly handsome young black actor in Los Angeles, calls his mime person Toy Man. "The name came to me first," he recalls, "then I said to myself, 'Now, how would Toy Man move?' And then I thought, 'Well, the Toy Man sits on a shelf most of the time, so he'd be still. And then at night, if he could, the Toy Man would come to life and he would do little things for you, and then he'd go back to his shelf.' " This scenario works very well on the Century City Mall, where Andre performs three days a week. In a tall red and white toy-soldier hat he poses for a few moments, then emerges in a wide-smiling, high-kicking strut to interact—picking an invisible flower for a child, creating a wall and peeking over it—then returns to his trance. Andre's freeze is extraordinary; a light is extinguished in his face to leave only the glittering eyes. "Dead" is too positive a word to describe the effect—it is almost as if he has ceased to be. "I just leave my body where it is for a while and kind of go inside," he explains.

His improvisations are limited by the conservative mall audience and its dynamics: "People are coming from work or going shopping, and they don't really feel like being bothered." Once in a while something interesting will break through: An elderly Jewish woman, a yenta, scolds him and pats his hand; another woman responds to his wall by building one of her own; they tunnel through to reach each other in a joyful reunion. "I wait for those moments," he said later. "On Saturday when the kids come I get to play."

Like many street mimes Andre is an actor waiting for the big break. He started out as a singer five years ago, has done a lot of legitimate theater and a few movies. His ambitions are wide—he wants to go to the top as an actor, then produce, while he carries on his mime show on the side. His formal training in mime was with Richmond Shepard, a Los Angeles teacher who has turned out many American mimes. Shepard, says Andre, studied to be a doctor, so he knows "exactly where the body breaks. He teaches it piece by piece, and that meticulous breakdown becomes a beautiful, peaceful flow in motion."

Training is important, but sometimes a sense of play can be almost as good. A mime who can touch the child within, who can abandon the dignity of the adult for the far more serious business of playing, can be entrancing. Late one night at Fisherman's Wharf we came across Bob Bennett, a young aspiring mime who, after his day's work as a telephone lineman, had come out on the street to play. In traditional whiteface, with one eye darkened in a triangle, he drew a large circle of people into his imaginary landscape and transformed the concrete and glass of the Anchorage arcade into a magic forest. Squatting grotesquely, with flickering tongue, he became a frog, seeking a kiss from a maiden. He chose his princess—my gray-haired photographer, Alice—got his kiss, and before our very eyes was changed into the handsome prince. Scooping her up while she giggled helplessly, he galloped off with her on a magic charger while we all clapped with glee. Three young toughs with beer cans came to scoff ("Hey, look at the weirdo fag!") and stayed to play when Bob handcuffed them and led them off to an invisible jail. They shook the bars, rattled the door, and then kicked a hole in the imaginary wall and escaped, looking pleased but a little embarrassed. A tall pole was a challenge to Bob's gymnast training; he ran at it and vaulted twelve feet up to the top where he balanced at an angle on one hand, his white-painted face conveying terror and surprise. Even a taxi became his plaything, as he brought one to a screeching halt by throwing himself before it on all fours, snorting and pawing like an enraged bull.

A trained mime who retains this sense of playfulness can create wonderful moments of unexpected delight on the street. Paul Dion plays with the crowd at the Metropolitan Museum entrance in New York. His audience sits on the stairs to watch while he gambols about involving passersby, policemen, and even cars and buses in his in-

Paul Dion mimes a perfect 36 on the Metropolitan Museum steps

stant theater. With wit and grace he mimics anyone foolish enough to cross his circle, then pretends to lasso a bus
and is dragged by it, and, chagrined by his failure, loops
the nonexistent rope over a traffic light and hangs himself.
Taking advantage of a lull in the traffic, he builds a wall
in the middle of Fifth Avenue. Becoming a monkey, he
leaps onto the hood of a taxi to sit grinning and scratching.
A car pulls to a stop at the curb; Paul skips up and opens
the door with a deep bow to lead the applause for the
sheepish and quite ordinary museumgoer who steps out.

When the crowd has been drawn into his scenario, he climbs the stairs among them, choosing volunteers with a pointing finger of glad recognition. He arranges twelve or fourteen people in a row and leads them in a weight-lifting charade, piling on the heavy stones as they crowd together to hold more and more aloft and finally spontaneously agree to heave it all onto Paul as he stands directing their efforts. All of this is done precisely, with elegance and control. The playfulness that in Bob Bennett's hands seems childlike is transformed by Paul Dion into art.

Although he is undoubtedly one of the three or four best street mimes in the United States, Paul's show-business aspirations are not in that direction. "It doesn't interest me at all; it's a means of getting somewhere right now." He came to New York from his native Massachusetts to be an actor, began studying mime between acting jobs, and then pursued it to Paris, where he was a student of Ella Jaroschewicz, the former wife of Marcel Marceau. He is currently studying with Stella Adler in New York. Paul has done mime in Europe, and finds audiences the same everywhere: "Mime has no language barriers," he points out. At the Metropolitan steps he alternates with comic Marc Wiener, the two of them passing the hat together. They make an adequate living at it, working only Saturdays and Sundays, and are free to pursue their theatrical objectives the rest of the week. There are other advantages, too: "We've gotten a lot of press out here, and that's a thing that helps career growth. Besides, you can really come out here and raise hell. We have a good time."

Another famous New York mime-performer, perhaps the most famous, is Philippe Petit. He would not define himself as a mime. He prefers to be known as a street juggler, or perhaps a funambulist or rope dancer. But his elegance of gesture and his near-silence bring him closer to the art of Debureau. "If he does speak," says circus-skills teacher Hovey Burgess, "it's a point of opposition to the fact that he doesn't usually speak. One time the police came and took him out of his circle in the middle of his performance and he came back and did a pantomime about how all the people in the park didn't like noise. He had the whole audience miming applause."

Petit begins his act by drawing a chalk circle about twelve feet in diameter to define his imaginary stage. Within it he rides a unicycle, juggles a bit, does some sleight of hand—all within a framework of mime. "He'll bring someone out and presumably teach them to juggle, and putting their hand in the right position to grab their wrist he sneaks off their wrist watch, and when they go back he'll hold it over their head," says Burgess. Petit is French, and has performed in the streets of most of the world's cities. Most Americans remember him as the daredevil who walked a wire between the two towers of the World Trade Center. Nowadays he ties his rope between a tree and a lamppost in Central Park.

The mime-character of Jack Albee is a literary construct. Jack is the cousin of playwright Edward Albee, and grew up in Paris among the absurdists and existentialists of the thirties. Jack Hemingway was his playmate, and as two mischievous kids they dubbed Gertrude Stein "Dirty Gertie" behind her back. In the sixties Jack, who was by then living in Los Angeles, was asked to produce an original costume character for The Pataphysical Circus, first of the theme festivals that later grew into the Renaissance Faire. He combined his early memories of the Fratellini Brothers clown act, the films of Giulietta Masina, and the early work of Marcel Marceau, and came up with a Pierrot-like character that was unique for that time. The creation was well received, and he found he felt comfortable in it. The mask of paint provided a refuge; a key element in the early formation of Jack's mime character was his conviction that words were dangerous. Silence seemed safe—if he said nothing he could not be criticized.

A year or so later he again donned the makeup and costume to distribute posters for the first Renaissance Faire, and when his armful of posters was all gone, he continued to cavort in the streets. Such a thing at that time was, of course, unheard of, but the decade was receptive to public craziness. Jack took his mime persona to San Francisco, where he performed with the accompaniment of a musical trio of violin, harp, and bass, and later joined forces with pioneer street-mime Robert Shields. The Cannery welcomed this new form of theater. But soon he was back in Los Angeles, where he settled in on the terrace of the County Art Museum. That was nine years ago, and he has been a fixture there on Sunday afternoons ever since.

Jack is not entirely sure that what he does is mime. He often talks; he explains the history of mime and gets a group of people up to act out an ancient Greek chorus; he tells a story while three or four children delightedly play all the characters; he composes abstract poetry of wordless sounds and fits motion to it. His performance area is strewn with props and toys for creating stories. His show is never the same twice, and he is endlessly fascinating to watch. Like all street performers, his ego is on the line every time: "Before the show today thoughts like this go through my head (as they did the first day): Do I have anything? Am I any good? Does it work? Will it work again?" But Jack has learned to use his inner psychological state to his own benefit. "Whatever mood I come out in I use during the performance—angry, sad, confused . . . The only emotion that isn't useful is if I have no energy and am very tired." During the week he paints, does children's birthday parties, makes ends meet however he can. His space on the Art Museum Plaza has been a nurturing place for many young mimes; he calls them his family. He has no other.

Some mimes are direct descendants of the silent film clowns. There are a number of Charlie Chaplin imitators among buskers—notably Samir Kamoun, who does his cane-twirling outside Chasen's Restaurant in Los Angeles. Jim Moore of New York calls himself a silent performer rather than a mime, and while his act is not specifically based on any one film figure, it is reminiscent in style of the great age of movie comedy. Jim arrives on his street corner dressed with shabby gentility in formal frock coat and white gloves, carrying a battered violin case. With prissy inexpertise he struggles an intractable folding music stand into position. Preparing to play, he peels off first one glove—it disappears (up his sleeve)—and then the second. It emerges, and emerges, and emerges in yards and yards of glove. Tucking an imaginary violin under his chin, he draws the bow across the strings, and real music is heard. The violin soon takes on a life of its own, repeating the same phrase over and over in spite of Jim's efforts to stop it. At last he whips out a pistol and shoots it dead, then, aghast at what he has done, lays a flower on the case and exits mourning.

SUGGS AT HOME

She had given us the address over the phone quite clearly, but I still am surprised. The house is an exquisite San Francisco Victorian, newly restored, with all of the lovely gingerbread scrolls outlined in their original brilliant and joyous colors. Carol Sue Thomas answers the door—a tall, delicate-boned woman with pale brown curls pinned artlessly up off her long neck. The lack of makeup does nothing to obscure her natural beauty. Inside, the house is even more handsome—gleaming hardwood floors, tall, narrow windows, a carved fireplace. "I just bought it recently, so I'm still fixing it up," she says to explain the sparse furnishings. We sit at the dining room table, and she clears away the clutter of papers and books on finance to make room for a photo album. "I've been studying for an exam," she says. "It's nice to have a break." We look at pictures of Suggs the Mime at work on the street and trace the development of the character. The costume is black and white with a touch of red—a heavy felt tunic. Carol Sue takes it out of the closet to show us. "Suggs is female, you see, but not feminine."

We speak of the differences between working the open spaces of Ghirardelli Square and the enclosed platform at the Cannery. "Let me show you how Suggs gets the stage ready at the Cannery." She beckons us into her studio. We sit on the floor and she indicates the mime movements with graceful, exact gestures. "I begin by mopping the stage floor." She picks up an invisible push-mop and works at it. Then she raises unseen posts at the four corners (asking for help on one that is especially heavy) and lifts the crossbeams into place. She pretends to drag a heavy trunk onstage ("I get a child to push on the other end") and opens the lid to peer in. Carefully she lifts out fabric; her undulating hands show us that it is filmy curtains. She shakes out the dust, sneezes, hangs them from the crossbar. Then, with innocent narcissism, she pretends to make up elaborately in a hand mirror, surveys herself approvingly, and, brushing aside the curtains, steps forward with assurance as—"Suggs the Mime!" A bow straight from the commedia—swashbuckling, hand on sword hilt, but with the swooping grace of the curtsy. In her empty hand is a velvet hat with a long, curving plume.

Mime is the only street art that attracts solo women performers in any number. The inherent androgyny of the mime and the power of the white face provide a protective façade that counteracts the vulnerability of the woman alone. The streets of San Francisco have nurtured at least two topnotch women mimes: Toad and Suggs. Toad (Antoinette Attell) was one of the pioneers, the performer who followed Jack Albee's early busking efforts at the Cannery. She made her reputation on the street and is now too busy touring and doing stage and television to be seen often there. Suggs, too, is one of the Old Boys. Under her real name, Carol Sue Thomas, she was a professional model, one of the first women to pose for ski magazines. As a child she was a dancer and an athlete, and "I was always a show-off. I remember as a kid I used to make my own puppets, my own stage sets, and the kids would come through my mom's kitchen and down into the basement and I used to put on my own productions." Carol Sue turned that theatrical flair to good use when she retired as a model. She studied for four years with Leonard Pit of the Berkeley School of Mime and with Ann Dennis Yankivitch, both Decroux mimes, and later she perfected her art with Sam Avital at the Center of Silence in Boulder, Colorado.

Suggs developed over a period of time as Carol Sue worked with the character on the street. Like many mimes, she feels that her mime persona has deep roots in her own hidden aspects, but that it is a separate personality. As we talked I would explore Carol Sue's thoughts on a subject and then ask, "How does Suggs feel about that?" Often Suggs's opinion was quite different. We spoke about the transformation that takes place when a mime prepares for performance by putting on the costume and white makeup. "When I put on that face, I really commit myself to that character," she said.

The techniques and the material that Suggs uses vary with the situation: one approach for open street scenes, another for the outdoor stages, and a third for indoor concert settings. On the big wide-open space of Ghirardelli Square plaza she warms up the area and takes possession of it only very gradually. "A mime can be threatening," she observed, "and Suggs is very powerful." She involves the spectators just a bit at first—a look, a wave, a gesture. Then she moves into small interactions: She listens to a fat stomach, unscrews and tries on heads, imitates people. Next she might draw them into a larger scene—a tug-of-war, a baseball game—finding the bat or the rope in unlikely locations like purses and pants legs. Sometimes Suggs becomes a robot—a gear meshes with a tremor as her torso turns, an eyelid flutters and clinks shut . . . Suggs exults in involving people in her world. "They get out there and get so high! I give them permission to play, and they've forgotten that." However, the mime must use that power responsibly. "One of the really important things is never to leave anybody undone. Even if you made a total fool of them, it's important to let them know that you really love them, and they were great—by a touch, or a hug, or giving them a bow."

On the Cannery stage, she uses less audience-involvement but is able to do more extended pieces. After a prologue to establish the character, she acts out little scenes, writing the title on a blackboard. Often she will ask for subjects from the spectators; one of her all-time favorites was "Moose in Love."

Recently Carol Sue did a one-woman concert of mime theater pieces. For the first half she used the traditional mime cards, but to satiric effect. Her opener, for instance, was "The Destruction of the World," followed by "The Destruction of Oakland." "The Wall" was a parody of that mime cliché. In the second half she dispensed with whiteface and used costumes and props to present a series of character studies of women: "Tess the Bag Lady" (in a red clown-nose), "Vogue" (a glimpse of Carol Sue the model), and "Telephones" (a surrealistic dance-impression of the demonic demands of Mr. Bell's invention).

The contrast between mime and clown is brought into sharp relief when the two work together. Historically, they share origins in the commedia dell'arte, but from there they diverge. Clown is actually the name of a character in the English pantomime, and his characteristic appearance was influenced by such great comedians as Joseph Grimaldi and, later, the Fratellini Brothers. In the last century the circus has been the primary theater for clowns, and in America their silence is an accident imposed by the size and turbulence of the three-ring extravaganza. There are several subtypes of clowns. The auguste wears no makeup in Europe but in America appears with a red rubber nose and white around the eyes and mouth only; he is the stupid and clumsy butt of the jokes of the more elegant and clever whiteface clown (Bozo, for example). A third, characteristically American, type is the tramp clown, as exemplified by Emmett Kelly.

A mime and clown pair that uses the two styles as comic foils without losing the integrity of either is Barbara Knight and Coco Leigh. They hold children spellbound in Central Park with a skit about a statue and a statue-painter. Mime Barbara, as a zaftig Venus, is in need of painting, and Coco, as a dedicated but inefficient work-person, arrives to do the job. In a rusty voice she an-

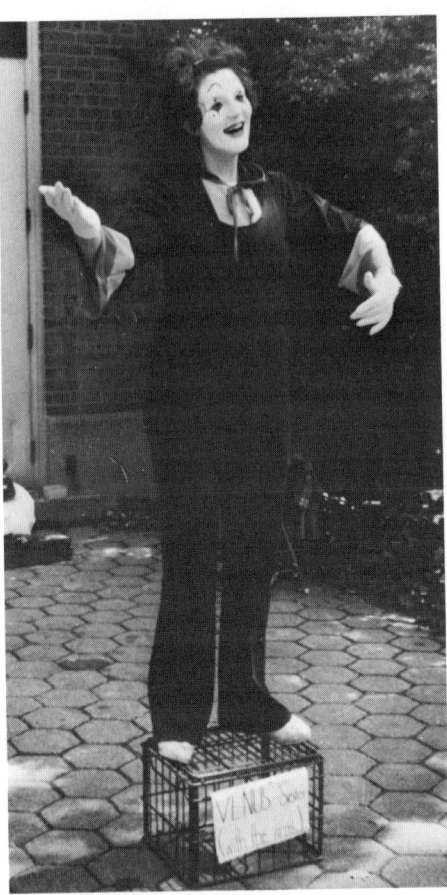

Small ones are enchanted by Barbara and Coco in Central Park.
Right: The Painter Painted

nounces her intentions and goes to work at it, while the statue shifts position and steals the bucket or the brush whenever the painter turns her back. Time out for a clown lunch leads to some funny business with a huge prop grapefruit. Back to work, and the children begin to shout "Look there! She's moving! Catch her now!" The scene ends in mayhem, with the painter painted, much to everybody's satisfaction.

The street partnership of Barbara and Coco is fairly transitory, although they were friends in high school and do well financially as buskers together. Barbara is "primarily an actress. I started studying mime to improve my

acting ability, and I find I've been making money at it."
She is in a mime company at her acting school and gets
booking through that connection for parties and other
shows. At first she worked alone on the street, doing mime
haircuts with children and other improvisations, but has
more fun with her clown partner. Coco is a graduate of
the Ringling Bros. Clown College and has worked in
circuses. "I've been interested in comedy since I was a
little kid. I thought that clowning was like the basis of all
comedy. Ultimately I would like to end up in some form
of stand-up or situation comedy," she said, her serious
expression contrasting oddly with her round red nose and

floppy carrot-colored wig. Both feel that women make better clowns because they have a natural rapport with children, and their own performance supports that assumption.

Clown-mime Alexis Lee combines the two styles in one person. She wears her waist-length brown hair in French braids around her delicate face, and exaggerates her eyes and mouth and cheeks with paint, although she doesn't use the traditional whiteface. In black leotard, a little jacket, and a floppy hat she is not as grotesque as a clown, but not as formal and androgynous as a mime. She begins her show in mime style, posing in a freeze with her hat set out, but then moves into typical clown bits—"I used to have this horn, and I'd go up to people and pretend I was going to pinch their noses, and honk the horn." She uses her voice in the act, reciting poetry and joking in an English accent. She also eats fire and does a bit of juggling to spice up the comic turns.

Alexis became a clown almost by accident. A woman friend wanted to take a course in clowning but didn't want to go by herself, so Alexis went along and very quickly found she loved it. She had been living in Atlanta and working as a Montessori teacher—"I was real stable" —but when a juggler friend showed her the different life of the streets, she was intrigued and eventually set out to seek her fortune. New Orleans and Key West have been her bases, although she travels freely. It has not been easy for a woman performer alone. "The times when I really needed the money and it wasn't coming back I had a real hard time." Alexis is still not making her entire living on the street; she does figure modeling for art classes to add to her income, and feels that the poses help her mime performance.

Alexis is young and small and pretty, and I wondered if she found the streets a dangerous place, especially honky-tonk Bourbon Street after dark. "The first night I went to work alone on Bourbon I was really scared! Because I had heard about all the drunks and mean ladies. But I am in control when I am my clown, and no one hassles me. I had one guy in Key West who scared me a little bit. First he came around and gave me a hug and then he started to lift me. And at first I thought, 'He doesn't know what he's doing; I could get hurt!' But as soon as he really started lifting I realized he knew what he was doing. He just lifted me straight up and I held the pose and he walked me around the crowd—I mean, it made the show, you know? Another time a guy put a cigarette in my hand when I was a mannequin and was moving my arm like I was smoking, and all of a sudden he turned the cigarette around so I burned myself. So I just let it drop out of my fingers without moving." In a way, Alexis's vulnerability is her protection and spectators will rally to help her. "One place on Bourbon a cop came up very nicely and told me that that was one spot that was off limits—all the owners on that corner really didn't like street performers. And then after the cop went away all the people came up to me and they were ready to fight the cop." But her best protection is the face itself, the distance and power of the fool. "I found nobody bothers a clown!" Sometimes she even takes the trolley home at two in the morning. "I walk anywhere alone myself, and it's so much easier to walk as a clown. If you get in a bad situation, you just clown your way out of it."

Sometimes mimes and clowns become entranced with that power and find that being behind the face is so safe that they never want to come out. Blossom, a traditional whiteface clown, has knocked about with his comical fire-eating act for many years. He gets up in the morning, shaves, and puts on his white paint and red rubber nose.

His fellow buskers at Jackson Square would never recognize him in ordinary flesh.

Russell Johnston, known as Rusty the Clown, agreed with Alexis that a mime/clown can do anything and get away with it. He has had a chance to test that belief in his far-flung travels. "I've done a lot of strange gigs," he says, among them rodeo clowning ("very dangerous; you have to be an acrobat"), acting as a goal post at car races ("they try to brake just two inches away from your nose"), and enlivening children's wards in hospitals. Alexis, too, has done her share of strange gigs; she once served briefly as a target for a knife thrower. "What did it feel like?" said I, agog. "Well, it was a rush, I'm telling you," she said, shaking her lovely head.

Rusty is unique as a clown because he has a long, bushy red beard. He explained his makeup: "I shave it down in here and here and do a sad face with just a dip of white and a tear and a red dot on the nose." His face is registered at the Pueblo Clown College, he said, a protective service that allows clowns and mimes to sue imitators. He has considered himself a clown since he was eight years old, when he became the bane of his teacher's life by imitating Jerry Lewis in class. There are many opportunities for clowns and mimes in commercial promotion, and Rusty is now working for an agency that hires him out for grand openings and trade shows and conventions.

Shoppers who stop to enjoy the antics of Dicken the Clown-Juggler in a mall in Binghamton, New York, or in Buffalo or Syracuse would be surprised to know that he is a college professor on sabbatical. Richard Cuyler, Dicken's real person, teaches in the Department of Theater at the State University of New York at Binghamton. "Clowning keeps me sane," he says. "Malls are big, cold, impersonal spaces. I want to bring smiles to people's faces," he rhymes.

Cuyler has been a student at the Clownshop held in Maine every summer by former Ringling teacher Fred Garver and Bob Berkey. "It's sort of a graduate clown school," he explains. He has also studied with Tony Montanaro at the Celebration Mime Theater in Maine—a school frequently mentioned by the best performers. In addition to the more commercial and highly competitive Ringling Bros. Clown College, another learning place is Carlo Manzzone-Clementi's Dell'arte School at Blue Lake, California. Mimes and clowns have no national organization at the present time that compares with the International Jugglers' Association, but a loose network has been cooperating around the project of an annual National Mime Week, and has centered in the Los Angeles Mime Guild.

No discussion of clowns and mimes on the street would be complete without the mention of two marginal phenomena: the balloon-sculptor clowns and the San Francisco Mime Troupe. Neither are true buskers. The balloon clown, although a common part of the street scene where tourists with children congregate, is not a performer but a merchant. He wears the makeup but usually has no skills in clowning; he twists balloons into animal shapes and sells them to those who have stopped to watch the process. The San Francisco Mime Troupe and other guerrilla theater originating in the sixties were and are primarily political advocates, although they performed in the streets and parks of cities and were innovators in opening up those areas. If money is collected it will be primarily for the furtherance of the political ideas that are being dramatized. The true busker, who depends on the support of *all* of his potential audience for a living, cannot afford to risk alienating some of them by espousing a controversial cause, no matter how worthy.

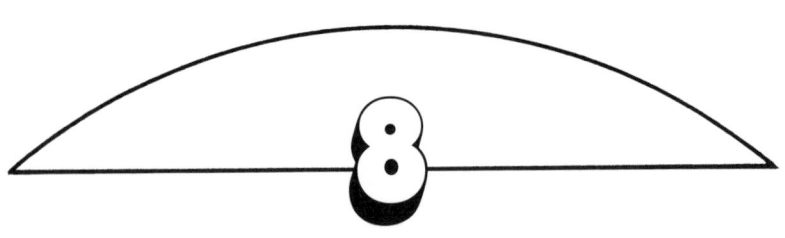

8

COMEDIANS AND OTHER FAST TALKERS

"How do we know Jesus Christ was Jewish?" asks Swami X, peering down from atop his park bench like a grizzled bird of prey. "Because he went into His Father's business." His audience, lolling on the grass among their bicycles and dogs, chortles and claps. This is what they are here for—to listen to the foul-mouthed sage of Venice plumb hypocrisy out of the depths of darkest respectability with his tools of profanity, blasphemy, and obscenity. "Know how to become a great leader? Hang out with desperately lost people. Story of *my* life." And he is off, attacking every national hero and sacred cow within flailing distance: motherhood, fatherhood, marriage, virginity, both political parties, organized religion, Billy Graham Crackers, Harvey Krishman . . . Violence, pomposity, and sham are his targets, and the salvation he preaches is love—but he spells it with an *F*. In a gravelly New York accent he lauds the virtues of that most basic of human activities in colorful and startling detail. The nice middle-class matrons, the vacant-faced fraternity boys, the chic roller skaters roar with pleased shock and delighted outrage. Swami can say anything. And does.

Obviously his act is not translatable to concert stage or television—or even nightclubs. He revels in the vulgar, the unsayable, the spontaneous verbal wrestling with the madmen and saints who flock to heckle. The street is his proper arena, and he knows it. For Swami is a holy man, a guru of grossness. Twenty years he spent as a disciple of Swami Sivananda. In 1968, at the age of thirty-nine, he left the ashram and chose the sidewalk for his pulpit, beginning on Telegraph Avenue in Berkeley and soon coming south, where he picked the boardwalk of Venice as his stage because, as local historian Sweet William says, he needed an audience that would be hard to please and easy to insult.

Off the bench Swami is shy and quiet-spoken, a little sad. He lives a simple life with his lady Sher, a serene and exotic beauty who looks like a gypsy princess but is actually a nursery school teacher. They do tai chi and yoga and ride their bicycles on the beach, and are both intensely interested in astrology. Swami will immediately take out a little book of astrological charts and analyze the potential of anyone to whom he is introduced. The Swami's name and past life are a mystery; if anyone is tactless enough to ask, he covers the faux pas by pretending not to hear. A paradox: a blasphemous mystic, a nameless celebrity.

New York, and especially Washington Square Park, seems to be fertile ground for verbal comedians. There Charlie Barnett works, like Swami, on the teetering edge of the shocking and the unmentionable, his material the embarrassments of small, unspoken racial tensions. He hurls himself across the Square, raging with exploding energy. "I don't have to do this for a living—I don't have to do this shit! I could be somewhere *robbing your fucking house!* I realize a lot of you white guys never been in a black guy's house—well, relax! Nine times out of ten we been in yours!" The crowd, mixed black and white, roars. "I notice the difference in the way different nationalities roller-skate," he says, and does a series of ethnic impressions on wheels: white, Chinese, Puerto Rican. Crouching over and swinging his arms wildly: "Black folks skate like they just stole something!

"I do a lot of ethnic humor, and people ask me am I prejudiced. Well, let me be honest with this audience: *I'm not black!* This is a birthmark! But let me be really honest. I don't think people hate one another because of the color of their skin—I think people just don't understand one another. Because everybody does stuff different." Lending money, for instance. "Puerto Ricans do it like this: 'Okay, bro, you see my knife? You see my thumb?' *Chop!* 'I just cut my thumb off—so you *know* I don't give a fuck about your head!' " Or transistor radios on the subway: "White folks hate it when niggers get on the train with them big goddamn radios! Honkies get mad as shit; they say:" (in a prissy voice) " *'Will* you turn that goddam thing off!' They go in the other train and call you names: 'You black bastard! You Alabama wartmonkey!' Niggers don't get on the train with no little bitty radios—when niggers get on the train, everybody has to wait while they put speakers up in the corners!"

Charlie has developed his violent style and his no-place-to-hide material on the street, and he has a devoted following in Washington Square. Howard Smith of *The Village Voice* tells of watching his first performance as a teen-ager: "About four or five years ago one of the comedians, who had become friends with him, had a big crowd and said, 'Why don't you come up and try it, Charlie?' He went up there and he made thirty dollars in about twenty minutes, and said, 'Well, I guess I can do this!' " He worked hard to improve, using a tape machine for self-criticism. Now he is about to make the transition to night-club comic, and will soon be lost to the open democratic hurly-burly of the streets.

Stand-up comedians who use only their voices are rare in busking. Many magicians and jugglers, as we have seen, are peddling laughter as well as wonder, but the performer who attempts to stand up on a box or a bench and hold a crowd with his bare wit has no recourse to props. He must not only have leather lungs and a sure fund of bits and routines, but he must also be able to meet the surprises and emergencies of the street with ready improvisation. And he must be willing to risk his ego; few things are as demolishing to a performer's self-approval as comedy that flops.

For these reasons many comics bolster their street acts with a bit of juggling, a bit of magic, or a bit of mime. Sean Morey's political juggles we have already described. Sean also does a couple of magic tricks that turn into sight gags: tucking a scarf like a bib into a woman volunteer's neckline, he performs a complicated egg-vanish on her head, and then whisks off the scarf—and a bra. But Sean's real strength is his ability to make comedic gold out of unexpected situations: a belligerent shopping-bag lady, a persistent dog that wants to play ball, an invasion of his circle by skateboarders. This flexibility gained on the street, along with his masterful timing and boyish charm, have brought him more and more show business opportunities in television.

SEAN MOREY WARMS UP THE CROWD

"Show time!" cries Sean. A few people stop to watch. "Now, we're going to play NAME THAT TUNE!" He whips a small harmonica out of his pocket and plays three vague notes. "Who can guess that tune? Come on, anybody!" He plays four notes, just as formless. "If you know the answer, just step right here into the circle and take your clothes off!" No response, but a lot of people have stopped now. He plays five notes this time, and a pretty girl on roller skates cries, "Star Trek!"

"Right! Come over here and get your prize!" (Cries of "Take your clothes off!" from the back row). The girl blushes and tries to hide behind her boyfriend. Sean takes a balloon out of his prop suitcase. "For knowing the answer, you get a balloon animal of my choice." He starts to blow it up. No success. He gives up and hands her the limp rubber finger. "There you are, a worm! Now, will you keep the worm, or do you want to go for the prize behind Ocean Number One?" He gestures expansively toward the beach. There are shouts from the now large crowd of "The worm! The worm!" She nods.

"Okay, so let's see what you would have won!" The sweep of his arm takes in the horizon. He shades his eyes and peers out to sea. "Aha—Hawaii!"

He turns suddenly on a tiny black poodle that has been yapping at him from the sidelines. "Run, Toto, run!" he cries urgently.

Sean's former partner, Marc Wiener, is also on the verge of graduating from the streets of New York to film and acting. In addition to the comic juggles that he and Sean shared, Marc does a variety of improvised mime bits with pedestrians, dogs, baby carriages, or whatever passes by. His bulging eyes and wild manner give his comedy a surrealistic air; he is given to strange characters and props, as when a rubber hand takes on a life of its own and chokes him slowly to death on the sidewalk. Marc has formally trained in mime and clown with Tony Montanaro of the Celebration Mime Theater in Maine. In his nightclub act he uses more costumes and even puppets to expand his repertoire of laughter. Marc's street theater is at the foot of the Metropolitan Museum steps in New York, a spot he occasionally shared with Robin Williams before that comedian became famous as Mork.

The Shakespeare Brothers are a two-man verbal act that defies classification. Both Alan Krulick and Steve Aveson are trained actors, tall, well-spoken men in their early thirties, who have done a great deal of legitimate theater of all kinds, including forays into radio and television. They perform on the street because they love it. In the summer they can be seen in Harvard Square in Cambridge, or at Quincy Market in Boston. When winter comes, they go their separate ways, touring with dramatic companies or puppet theaters, retreating to New England to write new comedy material. But when spring brings out the sidewalk strollers, they are back together on the street, delighting huge audiences with their own improvised theater of the unexpected.

A big steamer trunk is the center of their circle—overflowing with odds and ends of costumes and props. They might begin by waving long banners on sticks—a device seen in medieval drawings—while they comment on the news of the day ("Get your Pope paraphernalia here!" they cried on the day before that dignitary visited Boston. "Get your Pope cookies, your Papal turnovers, your hug-me, squeeze-me Pope dolls!" At the next show they took turns singing an oratorio about the Boston Red Sox's latest fiasco). Or Steve might do a bit of fire-juggling, or Al might dance with a marionette. "We get a crowd with visuals," they commented. "In order to get people to listen you've got to make them watch you first." When there are enough people gathered, they invite them to sit down, explain the rules ("Rule number two: When you leave please take all young people of the short persuasion with you—we have a closetful of them at home"), and launch into whatever zaniness appeals to them that evening. "We never do the same show twice," said Steve.

One night I watched them do a phony mind-reading routine straight out of vaudeville, a serious poem about saving the whales, and, in a later show, an improvised romp about springtime that used a dozen willing but bashful volunteers as trees, benches, and butterflies. For the mind reading, Al arrayed himself in a motley of sashes, feathers, and velvet beret from the trunk, and became— with a burlesque French accent—Monsieur Zogah! Steve, as his confederate, circulated among the audience and held up objects for the mind reader to identify—with the help of some outrageously transparent clues: "I hold up here for all to see—" ("I can see nah-zeeng!" complained the blindfolded Monsieur Zogah) "—an object!" He lifted a pair of glasses from a woman's nose and waved them aloft. "Now, Monsieur, *focus* on this problem. Do not fail and make a *spectacle* of yourself!"

"Zee object is—a pair of eye glazzes!" deduced the Frenchman, to thunderous applause.

The springtime skit was astonishing to watch as the brothers freed Bostonians in business suits to wave their arms overhead as trees or crouch as flowers and benches, cavort as butterflies. Later, when the playlet was finished and the principals were returning to the good-natured teasing of their friends, a dignified middle-aged woman who had impersonated a young lover passed by me. "I can't believe I did that!" she marveled to her husband, and there was a stunned look on her face. When I described the moment to Al later, he said, "We break, we attack people's preconceived roles. Steve has opened the lives of hundreds of people. We don't make fun *of* people though; we try to make fun *with* them. I don't recall ever insulting anybody. We do make people laugh at one another, because there's a lot of tightasses around. But we couldn't do it if they didn't give us the power to make them untightassed.

"We care a lot about doing things on the street that are verbal and thoughtful," he added. "So it's not just mindless, not just a spectacle." Steve offered a definition: "Zaniness with a theatrical bent and occasional purpose."

The Shakespeare Brothers' partnership and their name arose one afternoon five years ago when the two of them were the only members of a Shakespeare company willing to accept the invitation of a local block-festival to extemporize on the street. Since then they have taken their act to New York and Philadelphia, although they both feel strongly that Boston is the best place. In a burst of romantic wanderlust, Al attempted to travel the country as a busker several years ago, but "I barely got home alive." He found the streets of most of America were slim pickings. Steve is originally from San Francisco, where his first busking experience was as half of a bizarre act called Voodoo and Stefano—he read poetry while a woman partner tap-danced in toe shoes.

For a time Al and Steve worked with a third partner—a mime, who provided the visuals to their verbal badinage. He has gone on to fame and financial success, but, says Steve, "he misses the nurturing that he got from the contact in the street." This warmth and immediacy of reaction is the appeal of busking, they are convinced. "The street has the potential for reaching more people in one night in an intimate way than you can in a circus or in Las Vegas, because the quality of the contact is better than anywhere else. You fit five thousand people into a circus arena and you get next to no contact, because the closest people are three hundred feet away."

Steve spoke of the impetus to creativity that comes from that close interaction with the audience: "A lot of the routines that we do are like a big, loose-knit sweater. There's a lot of room in there for different gusts of wind to get through, for fingers to squeeze through and hug and things like that. The audience gives us the indication of what to expect—is it a gust of wind, is it a poke, is it a squeeze? And sometimes it's funny, and sometimes you tighten it up and bring it together faster, and sometimes you leave it open. When it's wide open it means the audience is really receptive and there's potential for new stuff to happen. A lot of our best bits have just appeared one night and we kept them. Something new happens every night."

"In what other medium do you have this freedom?" Al continued. "Not on TV or in nightclubs. There's no other place where we would have the power to say what we please, the way we want to. Out here I say what I like because I'm talking to human beings." The Shakespeare Brothers, like Will the Juggler, are mystical about the sense of involvement they create in their audiences: "Basically all street performers serve the function of creating community and bringing people together, and if we can take them a little bit further and have them recognize our mutual humanity, then it's like going to church, or the theater, or Thanksgiving dinner." Al brought it back down to earth: "This act could go over in any gutter in the country!"

Puppet theater has a long tradition in the streets. Punch-and-Judy shows have been a staple of the marketplace for hundreds of years. Steve Hansen and his partner Gary Schnell have found that audiences still cheer for the Crocodile and the Devil and still roar when Punch tosses the baby out the window. Their version of the old, old puppet play is embellished with contemporary asides, just as it must have been done long ago. They developed it for the Renaissance Faire but performed it also for several years in Aquatic Park in San Francisco. *Punch and Judy* is only one of the several plays in their repertoire; they have two shows together, and a collection of four one-man shows for a variety of different ages. Steve has also been seen on the streets of many cities with his ambulatory puppet theater: a box that fits around his upper body and allows him to walk while he performs.

At Ghirardelli Square I watched Gary do an adult puppet play starring shaggy dog Milton as the host of a radio show. Milton leered at pretty girls and invited them to meet him after the show to go down to the beach and roll in dead fish. A frog guest star bemoaned his transformation from a handsome prince and invited a maiden from the audience to give him the magical kiss that would lift the spell. A dumpy matron in polyester pantsuit was enticed up on the stage to do the deed, but afterward the frog was unchanged. "Well," decided Milton, "there's only one explanation: You ain't no maiden!" At the end of the show he passed his dog dish in lieu of a hat.

Both Steve and Gary are veteran buskers; Gary began in 1970 at Fisherman's Wharf, and Steve has played in the streets since 1968. The bulk of their income comes from fairs, but they also do a wide range of other gigs: festivals, conventions, private parties, elementary schools, and colleges. Steve was with the Muppets for two years, and Gary has traveled extensively with his own show; for a

Gary Schnell tidies Milton for the next show

Left: Milton wows a small fan

while he concentrated on the Financial District in New York and is very fond of downtown lunch-hour audiences. He works hard at his art—"I used to perform seven days a week for three hours every day. That may not sound like much, but there's a lot of energy involved. I used to come home just wiped out." His years of experience have given a sure command of audiences; he has learned how to set people up for lines that sound spontaneous. "I'm very seldom surprised," he said and then told me three surprising stories that appear in Chapter Eleven. I had thought that transporting the equipment for the puppet theater might be a difficulty on the street, but Gary showed me how it all breaks down compactly into two trunks on wheels. "The real street problem for a puppeteer is noise. You can't hear yourself when you're inside there, and you have to just hope that the amplifier is working."

While he talked, Gary brushed Milton's ears to tidy him for the next show. I was curious about the relationship between master and puppet, and asked if he thought of Milton as human. "Well, not really," he answered slowly. "But one time I was making a new Milton-puppet because the old one was wearing out, and I had to use the old eyes and nose. I laid him on the worktable, and I had to explain to him why I was doing it. Even then I felt sad when I threw him in the spare-parts box afterward."

Ventriloquists are even more aware of anthropomorphizing the dummy. David Strassman described the personality of his partner, Chuck Wood: "He's witty, abrasive, very intelligent, and wise. He has the mentality of a four-hundred-year-old (he's from a redwood) and sometimes the immaturity of a three-year-old. As for gender, he's tri-sexual—if it's sexual he'll try it. But seriously, I've been performing with him for ten years, and his reality has to exist for me or else *you* won't believe that he exists." Is he aware of Chuck's personality coming out of his own psyche? "His hostility is true. It's a great outlet for me. If someone is heckling me during the show, Chuck will come back with 'Why don't you go suck an exhaust pipe!' If people get mad at his insults he'll just look around and say, 'He thinks I'm real!' It only backfired once; this guy couldn't take it, and he slammed me up against a bank window and said, 'I'm going to push your head through this glass!' I said, 'Please don't do that!' and talked my way out of it. But usually this inanimate object can say anything he wants to anybody, and I can't get the blame."

Storytelling, although it has flourished in schools and libraries, has not yet been revived to any great extent as a street art. In Boston I heard about Brother Blue (Hugh Hill), a famous Boston street storyteller, who wears bells on his fingers and is surrounded by quivering butterflies on wires while he weaves his spell with words. He draws not only from the black oral tradition but from more literary sources, even Shakespeare, and his rendition of Macbeth is said to be one of the great street experiences. Brother Blue is no vagabond busker—he has a doctorate in religion, and his wife is a dean at a Boston college.

The only other storyteller that I encountered (besides juggler Jeff Chroman) was Jehan Clements, and he was only able to ply his craft in the parks and plazas of New York because he had the blessing of the Recreation Department and, later, a government grant. Nevertheless, he feels very much a part of the tradition, and even grew a beard to fit the image of the great storytellers: Johnny Appleseed, Rip Van Winkle, Paul Bunyan, Sholem Aleichem, and especially the Sufi bard Nasrudin. I wondered how he set up the necessary peacefully attentive audience. "I would go up to people with children and tell them that there's going to be some storytelling in five minutes over there under the tree, and give them my brochure." When he had gathered several people, he would start with an introduction about storytelling, play a tune on the recorder or sing a short song, and by then he had a group. He would tell tales for about twenty or thirty minutes, and then close with another recorder melody and a plug for his storytelling radio program on listener-sponsored WBAI. Jehan is every inch a teller of tales. His genial face is partially hidden behind a sandy, scraggly beard and bushy moustache, and his long hair is caught back by a rubber band. He wears sandals and a loose peasant shirt, and as he talks his hands move expressively and his eyes twinkle under shaggy brows. He favors the short wisdom tales of Nasrudin and Aesop, but some-times does stories of his own that reduce sophisticated city kids to happy giggles—"The Banana That Ate New York" is a favorite.

While storytellers are rare, poets are not too unusual on the street. But, like the balloon sculptors, they are usually merchants in the guise of performers, with the primary aim of selling mimeographed sheets of their own poems. An exception is Pagan the Poet, who has been a roving bard all his adult life. "I've done nothing to earn money but write and quote poetry since I was nineteen years old," he told the *Los Angeles Times*. Now thirty-two, Pagan Neil is a rotund, bearded man in baggy, faded tie-dyed pants; he carries a heraldic banner to announce his name and profession. He has a repertoire of twelve hours of memorized poetry, some of it his own compositions, and can reel off a poem to suit almost any request. His memory is phenomenal, and he claims to be able to retain a passage after only a few readings. His knack for obsolete vocabu-lary is put to good use at both California Renaissance Faires, where he plays the Shire Poet. Pagan was raised in Boston, but he has wandered the world with his recita-tions, including some areas where other buskers fear to tread. "In Jackson, Mississippi, I was told I had until dark to get out of the state," he recalled. "Another itinerant poet was shot on the street in Memphis, Tennessee." The *Los Angeles Times* quoted his further misadventures: "I've been beaten, mugged, and chased down back alleys by thugs. But," he shrugged, "there are critics everywhere."

A long line of theatrical wisdom, stretching from the medieval mystery plays to the commedia dell'arte to guerrilla theater, has decreed that broad comedy is what works best in the streets. A number of modern improvisation groups have reaffirmed this old truth. Ed Hauck and Bob Logan, leaders of a group called After the Juggler, summed it up: "On the street it has to be big—*blam boom*! It has to be more physical because voices don't carry as well and you're battling traffic noise and the elements. Indoors you can be more subtle and subdued and play it honestly." After the Juggler (so named because their space in Westwood is dominated by jugglers earlier in the evening) is a cyclone in action—all twelve members flinging themselves about their little circle acting out movie titles or popular songs or taking suggestions from the audience for improvisations on "your favorite emotion" or "a nervous mannerism." The members of the group enjoy their regular Friday-night outdoor performances, but they consider the wild sprawling comedy they do there as a preamble to their real purpose—to have a small theater or nightclub of their own. This dream has crystallized around a modest inheritance that came to Bob last year when his mother died. Left with no family, he advertised for other actors to join him in an improvisational group: "I've never really done a lot of comedy, and I've always wanted to. I love to laugh, and I just thought it would be neat to have our own little place where we would be able to laugh together and make enough money so that it would pay for itself—and maybe a little bit to help me out with my rent." So far their street appearances have brought them a little publicity and a little money—enough to hire a rehearsal hall and keep their dream warm.

Their aspirations are not without precedent. The L.A. Connection began on the streets, and now the fifty-member company leases a theater where their four groups perform on Friday and Saturday nights and where they teach acting classes during the week. They still value the street experience, however, and use it as practice for their student groups. "They learn how to project their voices, how to play to larger crowds, how to handle hecklers, and how to play to a wide variety of people—all ages and ethnic groups," said director Kent Skov. To protect the student groups from police harassment and arrest, Skov applied for a permit from the Venice Parks and Recreation Department to perform on the park lawn near the beach every Sunday afternoon. L.A. Connection, like After the Juggler, has a street repertoire of improvisation games that provide a structure for audience involvement and spontaneous creativity from the actors. "What It Is," for instance, is a wild-eyed quiz show in which the actors create a stable of dingbat contestant-characters and then use them to describe an object donated by the audience: A contestant lunges up to the mike wearing his sneakers sideways. "What is your name, sir?" asks the game show host.

"Clyde Tupperware!" he blurts happily.

"And what do you do, sir?"

"I do drugs! All the time!"

Skov, who is an alumni of The Committee and other former street groups, finds that the open-ended situation is valuable for an actor: "You're getting and giving at exactly the same time without any transaction financially.

If the audience wants to stay, they can, and if you want to perform, you can. No strings attached. There is immediate gratification—donations are something extra." In 1978 the company did a marathon 101 shows in fifty hours—some indoors, some radio, but mostly on the street. "I'm willing to go and play in any possible setting as long as they give a little bit of room to have the performers go."

Some street talkers have made a career out of a talent for being a loudmouth—Norbert Yancy of Ghirardelli Square, for example, who intersperses a few simple tunes on the guitar with insults shouted at passersby in any of twenty different languages. Mentalist Glenn Gazin even had training in loudmouth—he majored in rhetoric at the University of California at Berkeley. It was there that he was inspired by listening to Swami hold forth on Telegraph Avenue. Glenn calls himself a "street psychic"—the only performer with that specialty, he believes. A small, dapper man, he is bitter about his life as a busker. His face is sardonic as he describes his act: "Before the show I get the audience to write down questions on slips of paper and put them in envelopes. I collect them, and then I'll pick one up and tell the writer what the question is and answer it, showing amazing insight and humor. This is a show for the educated. I find the streets aggravating, because theater happens in the minds of the audience, and with all the distractions and noise it's very hard to maintain concentration." Glenn is about to bid the street goodbye: "I started here. Now I've been at it two years, and I work professionally. I feel a little bit ridiculous performing for nickels and dimes when I can get a couple hundred dollars a show. But it's great training, like isometrics. Whenever I give a show in a nightclub or at a party, I'm always amazed at how little relative effort gets tremendous response, laughter, interest. Being on the streets taught me to work in the very worst conditions." But he also had

Glenn Gazin gets ready to read some minds

political motivation for choosing the life of the streets even temporarily: "Part of the reason I'm doing this is that I really hate all authority. All authority is corrupt; I have great contempt for the system—especially civil service bureaucratic, institutional authority. I'm a monarchist-anarchist," he sneers. As for the spectators, "Applause is the most annoying sound in the world. My ideal audience pays tribute with an awed hush."

185

MADMEN, VISIONARIES, AND CIRCUSES
(And a Note on Dance)

The Human Jukebox has been called "the perfect street act." It can be seen at the top of Aquatic Park in Fisherman's Wharf—a tall canvas and wood structure about the size and shape of a telephone booth, decorated with crudely lettered instructions and lists of tunes. A coin dropped in one of the holes on the side of the box precipitates thumpings and stirrings, and then a flap at the front is jerked up and a trumpet is thrust out. A popeyed, bearded musician plays a snatch of the selected melody, and then, with a descending squeal from a Looney Tunes bird whistle, the flap falls abruptly closed. Occasionally, if the tourists are reluctant, the box will encourage them with growls of unintelligible political invective. Persistent photographers who neglect to sweeten the kitty will be confronted with an ancient box camera aimed out of the opening, and then the rebuke of the closed flap.

This cryptic performance draws a gaggle of giggling watchers from morning till night. Although it may be the perfect street act in terms of its attraction for tourists, it yields little satisfaction for the man who spends his days in the canvas cage. While other performers draw nurture and inspiration from the close contact with their street audiences, Grimes Poznikov has chosen to hide himself from them in paranoid seclusion.

An interview with Grimes is a strange and trying experience. Because he has been so often exploited by the media, his approach to a question is like that of a spider to an entrapped fly—he immediately coats it with layers and layers of weblike rhetoric, until it has no resemblance to the original shape. I asked him, "What does it feel like in there?" He answered, "I can't describe that! It varies according to the astrological situation at the time of day and the course of the moon; different things affect the mood situation. This is just like a regular gig, a form of mass psychotherapy—it's another fraud system."

He has been on the street with the Jukebox since 1973, but his first street experience was in 1968 at the Chicago Democratic Convention. While he was playing "America the Beautiful" outside Lincoln Park, "a guy stuck a gun up against my head and threatened to *blow my brains out*! I went and got convicted for mob action, and it was my first bust since I had grown up in Kansas and gone to college in Iowa. Getting handcuffed and maced while in the squad car and all these torture techniques I didn't know existed until I experienced them personally convinced me that street music is a context that I would utilize for a period of time. I went and got my degree in psychology and my interest in music therapy led me to formulate this Jukebox as a conceptual participatory street music system to allow

people to participate in changing their environmental scene so that it in effect dissipates motivations that cause such things as armed conflict, criminal activities, and the like. And the Jukebox in effect if deployed throughout the planet can effectively replace all tactical nuclear weapons and other such monstrosities." "I am on the interface between science fiction and reality," he pointed out accurately. He handed me a grubby card. It read "Society for the Advancement of Non-Verbal Communication. Division of Experimental Multi-Media Art Development. Grimes Poznikov, Consultant."

Grimes's longtime girl friend, Harmony Chadwick, confirmed that he did indeed grow up in Kansas, as one of the four children of a small-town lawyer. "He's sort of the black sheep," she said sadly. "His parents don't like what he's doing at all—no matter how many newspapers he's in." For a time before he was radicalized in the sixties, Grimes taught school in Chicago but "got fired for wearing a short-hair wig." He and Harmony met in Amsterdam in 1971, where Grimes had been existing by playing the trumpet casually on street corners and in parks. They traveled together, and the combination of their two unconventional personalities got them into a couple of tense situations with national authorities. Once they overstayed their visa in Czechoslovakia and were only able to pay the fine because the guard allowed them to play at the border until they had accumulated enough kopeks. Another time they lived underneath the Eiffel Tower for three days when their truck died there; the police, attracted by the sound of Grimes's trumpet, came to arrest them on the third day, but stayed to help them push the truck to a mechanic.

In San Francisco he and Harmony live in a reconstructed warehouse with sixty other artists. Growing disillusioned with the street, this year Grimes has returned to schoolteaching, although he still wheels the Jukebox out on weekends. Because there were no books issued to the students at tough, black Wilson High School, he has been taking them radical newspapers like the *Hipster Times* for relevant reading. "The kids like him fine," says Harmony.

A street performer herself, Harmony ("The Cosmic Cowgirl") does a rope-twirling dance to taped electronic "celestial" music. Her wealthy Maryland family bought her her first horse at ten so that she could join them in horse shows and riding to hounds. Sent off to an old, conservative college, she was soon in trouble for wild partying and became something of a campus celebrity when her activities led her sorority to be voted "Most Sociable of the Year." Settling down, she graduated in Recreation

Therapy and worked with returning Vietnam veterans at Philadelphia Naval Hospital, and later as a Vista worker in the ghetto. "I've worked with so many people who've been really messed up," she says. "Psychiatric wards, alcoholics . . ." After her European adventures she answered an ad for a woman rider to train for a Wild West act, and learned trick roping and riding. She was a sensation in the ring until the unlucky day when she fell from the horse and shattered the bones of her arm.

Grimes and Harmony occasionally perform together. The most notable occasion was their appearance on *The Gong Show*. Harmony walked up to the box, put a coin in, and said, "Play a Western song, Pardner!" Grimes popped out and tootled the "William Tell Overture" while Harmony spun her rope around the box. They were quickly gonged. "I don't like out-of-tune trumpets," said a judge. Grimes refused to accept this as nonpolitical music criticism. "I'll bet that guy saw me on the street and didn't like my rap," he grumbled.

The outer form of the Poznikov street act has been copied occasionally in other cities—a woman Jukebox performs in Central Park, a New Englander busks with a portable version, and two preteens crouch in a refrigerator carton on Venice Beach. The structure may spawn imitations, but Grimes's style and political rhetoric are his alone.

The Human Jukebox is rivaled in strangeness only by the Human Mannequin, Curtis Read. Although it is part of every mime's bag of tricks to pose as a mannequin, only Read puts himself into a catatonic trance as a normal condition of his working day on the street. Dressed to the teeth in one of several elegant outfits, he will choose a good spot (preferably in front of a store window with display dummies), pose, and go rigid. His heart slows to twenty-eight beats per minute, his flesh becomes white

Curtis Read, the Human Mannequin, poses in a catatonic trance

and cold, and the pupils of his unblinking eyes shrink to jiggling pinpoints. Foot traffic stops dead at the eerie sight, and the little leather case by his side is soon full of coins. Read claims that it took him six years to learn the secret "through yoga training." In Europe he holds the pose for as long as three hours, but American audiences are much more easily bored, so he is still for only a few minutes before leaping up with a sudden roar to lunge with his cane at a shrieking spectator.

Read was born in Switzerland and grew up on a farm school there (he told me), was born in Oakland to a couple who own several grocery stores (he told *People* Magazine), or is a native of Gainsville, Florida (he told a Swiss paper). He studied to be a forest ranger *(People)*, or learned mime at the University of Florida and worked as a store dummy (the Swiss paper), or spent some time in an army mental hospital *(People)*. Later he trained and rode alligators and became known as Gator Man at University of Florida football games *(People)*. What is certain is that he is thirty-one years old and has been a street mannequin for seven years. During that time he has traveled around the world twice, picking up such odd jobs as sitting motionless in a bath at Auckland's Easter Show, posing in a tank as G.I. Joe for a New Zealand Armed Services Day, or mingling with the wax effigies at Madame Tussaud's in London. Read is well received in Europe, but they are especially fond of him in Switzerland, where his arrival on June 1 in Lausanne is an annual event.

While he is in the trance, he says, observers often give in to the temptation to test his consciousness with nasty tricks: putting itching powder down his neck, pinching and hitting and stabbing, shoving fingers up his nose, undressing him, and even setting him afire. He just stands there. (When he was a child, he had told me, the other boys persecuted him because he was "different.") Women are apt to try different tactics, he said with distaste— "cute" things like hugging and kissing or giving him a flower.

At first glance Read looks quite ordinary with his square, almost-handsome face, broad snub nose, and close-cropped hair. Then it is impossible not to notice his light, deep-set eyes. "I have very scary eyes," he admitted to a *People* reporter. Read came to Hollywood with visions of a show business career, but now sees himself as reduced to working on the street to pay the rent because of lack of other opportunities (although he is vague when questioned as to what those "other opportunities" might be). However, he enjoys his work and is endlessly amused by the public reaction to his trances. Sometimes he even does it on the bus, leaning corpselike against his startled fellow-passengers.

David Landau, the Westwood Tumbler, is a self-defined madman. "You've gotta be crazy to do this," he said. I had wondered why there were almost no other acrobats on the streets, and David explained it. Tumbling on concrete causes ligament and muscle damage, and "nobody but a young punk would do it." David does it—every Friday and Saturday night in Westwood. Weighing all factors carefully, he chooses the best movie line for his purposes—he prefers older, more sophisticated (and richer) audiences—and arrives when the line stretches down the block. He goes up and down the curb with a brash, fast-talking spiel, building suspense. Gesturing toward the cars and buses whizzing by on Wilshire Boulevard, he proposes to do a triple flip down the middle of the street. At first they laugh, but gradually he convinces them that he really is going to attempt it. When anticipation has been built up to a peak and all eyes are on him, he catches a split-second lull in the traffic, takes a short run, and, unbelievably, flips and flips and flips right in the middle of the boulevard, missing cars by inches. Then he passes the hat quickly and beats a hasty retreat before the police can catch up with him.

Tightrope-walking is an ancient and glorious madness. Certainly the most spectacular recent outdoor exhibition of that madness was that dared by street performer Philippe Petit, when in 1974 he crossed seven times between the towers of the World Trade Center. Other funambulists stay closer to the ground. Bruce Smith of Central Park works at seven feet where, he claims, "it's not dangerous if you do only what is within your grasp. Ninety-five percent of the time you know when you've lost your balance, so you can jump before you fall." Bruce has more than balance to think about when he's performing; he plays bluegrass or Irish music while he's high overhead. In slim rolled trousers and mismatched socks (a personal superstition) he dances to his own accompaniment on the fiddle or the penny whistle or the tabor pipe, does the splits, and even stretches out for a nap on the wire. His pitch is poetic: "My only support is my rope and what I get in my fiddle case, so please leave a leaf, coins from any realm, a child, fruit in season . . ." Bruce has trained carefully for his act. He has a degree in dance and movement for the theater, and is now studying acrobatics and the high wire at the Circus Arts Center in Hoboken. After only one hour of instruction in the slack rope he mastered it alone by practicing in Central Park. Rope-walking has a long history as theater: The ancient Greeks did it between the masts of their ships, and during the golden age of the Théâtre des Funambules in Paris even serious plays like Hamlet were performed on the wire. Bruce would like to reawaken the public to the uses of the rope as an integral part of drama. Amazingly, fate seems to have presented him with an opportunity to achieve that ambition. This year he has a part in the musical *Barnum*, in which he sings, dances, acts—and walks on the wire.

There are some buskers who are on the street not as an expression of a talent or a love of performing, but because the life-style meshes with their personalities. Stan Sindberg is one of these. He has been a busker for two years; before that he did "all different kinds of odd jobs, basically anything that wasn't forty hours a week." Street performing appealed to him because it was "kind of on the fringes between the nine-to-five world and the derelict world—being fairly free and taking your own time and pace and place." He has put together an eclectic but derivative act, of which he says, "I play the guitar; I juggle; I do magic; I lay eggs . . ." In performance he is an ordinary Joe, a cheerful amateur, whipping through the Slidoni toilet-paper trick, the cigarette burn in the jacket, a few political juggles, a bit of the devil sticks, and winding up by teaching five volunteers a rudimentary disco dance while he bangs out a song of his own composition on the guitar. The act works because he brings to it a certain gusto and a flair for crowd control. "I don't put a lot of energy into developing it," he reveals, "because I don't plan to be doing this five years from now." But in the meantime he spent last year traveling and busking in Europe and makes an adequate living on the summer streets of his native Boston.

Other eclectic performers are truly multitalented, harking back to the versatile jongleurs, and such acts can be original and interesting. With experience and skill as a juggler, magician, and clown, Moonbeam of New Orleans is a busker's busker. Other French Quarter performers admire and emulate him and look forward to the days when he comes into town from his farm fifty miles up the river. Although he has only been a committed street performer for four years, his experience has been broad. In France he wrote for mime and traveled on the Continent as a clown-juggler. Returning to Boston, he studied mime in that city and taught juggling there. His performance image is Renaissance, and he prides himself on working only with objects that could have been used a thousand years ago. A spectacular skill unique to Moonbeam in this country is water-spouting. The trick has a long history as a traditional street act, he maintains. Filling his mouth with water, he promises to spout it forty times. While the audience counts he spews jet after jet into the air, going long beyond the promised forty and finishing stylishly by catching the last squirt in his outstretched derby hat. When he was traveling in Europe, his audiences loved it —except in Morocco. In that desert country water has always been a precious and respected commodity, and Moonbeam's flagrant wasting of it was greeted with shocked silence. A true professional, he quickly adjusted his patter to emphasize preserving rather than squandering.

A trend seems to be developing among many performers to accumulate a variety of skills or to join together with other multitalented buskers in troupes that are essentially small circuses. Bill Galvin (also known as Dr. Hot or R. Rufus Reefer) began in San Francisco as a juggler, but over several years has added comedy dialogue, whiteface, unicycling, magic, and rope-walking, not to mention several transient partners skilled in clowning, juggling, or banjo-playing. Like most circus-type acts he is an itinerant and has performed not only in the United States but also in the streets of South America.

Mountain Mime is a pair of delightful young mime-acrobat-jugglers from Vermont: Tom Murphy and Benj Marantz. They frisk through acrobatic tumbles, juggle, walk an imaginary rope, and perch on each other's shoulders to mime vast distances below. Tom seldom speaks, but Benj squeaks jumbled instructions in a terrified Mickeymouse voice. ("Higher!" he cries—and then, "Not so higher!" Smirking in satisfaction, he pipes, "Prrrrr-itty good, huh?" after a flashy trick.) Their ladies, Jeanne Wall and Linda Murphy, are about to join the act for some four-way juggling, and Jeanne sometimes does a modest belly dance on the slack wire.

The Slap Happys are one of the glories of Boston street theater. This eight-man act combines virtuoso juggling with broad visual comedy and the backing of a five-piece band. Juggler Allen Jacobs has mastered some astounding feats—among them a forward somersault ending in the chin-catch of a flaming torch. Their comic imagination is a triumph of nuttiness—a whip-cracking, wild-bike trainer subduing a herd of five furry bicycles, for example. But their most memorable stunt is a knee-high, abrasive, self-congratulatory character named Stubby Malone, who appears when comedian Tom Keegan and an invisible assistant reclothe and reassemble their arms to create the illusion of a misshapen, short-legged fellow in huge sneakers.

But of all the multitalented street ensembles, Loco-Motion Vaudeville are undoubtedly the most skilled, the most versatile, the most professional, and the most entertaining. The troupe is made up of three massive-shouldered clown-acrobats—Bounce, Cyrus, and Flip—and their resident intellectual, Jan Kirschner. Jan, who originally joined them to research his doctoral dissertation on street theater, does most of the talking onstage, juggles, and occasionally acts as straight man. The three clowns have welded their combination of talents into dozens of comic sketches; for any one performance they might choose only four or five of these from their huge repertoire. Not content merely to showcase their feats of juggling and acrobatics, they work them into a dramatic framework with its own dynamics and comedic motion. For instance, Cyrus escapes from a securely tied straitjacket while riding a tall unicycle, but he does it as the comic climax of a skit in which he impersonates a crazy-hip Beat poet from the fifties. Their hand-balancing tricks are spectacular pyramids and towers from which their bodies hang sideways in the air at impossible angles; their juggling is deft and original; their clowning and tumbling is a perfectly timed delight. Cyrus plays the accordion;

Bounce can do disciplined classical mime; Flip's whiteface slapstick approaches the best work of the great Red Skelton. And all of this is blended into a seamless theatrical piece that leaves their audiences gasping and laughing.

Offstage Bounce's traditional triangular hairdo (bald in the middle, high and wild on the sides) marks him instantly as a clown, but his demeanor, by contrast, is sober, even a bit stern. Driving up to Marblehead for a street fair in his equipment-crammed van, we spoke of his weariness with life on the road. "Twenty thousand miles last year," he sighed. His dream would be to have a small theater for the company. Loco-Motion does a stage show on the college circuit in the winter and summers in Boston, where they are regulars at Quincy Market and the many New England fairs. They also spend some of the winter months in Key West, where Bounce has a house. All three men have big live-in vans in which they stow their many props, backdrops, and acrobatic paraphernalia. But even with their consummate professionalism they are not beyond doing a spontaneous show on a likely street corner when the impulse takes them. They are vaudeville street performers, they stress, and not a circus.

———————————•———————————

THE CIRCUS IN THE ALLEY

A red and yellow circus ring is waiting in the grease-stained alley behind the Catholic Worker Hospitality Kitchen in downtown Los Angeles. People are waiting too—Chicana mothers with babies, shambling derelicts and winos, strange loudmouthed old women, and tall, healthy college kids aproned for their work in the

Kitchen. The buildings—abandoned apartment-hotels with dead, black windows—the alley, the people, are gray with hard times and sad days. The only color in all this scene is the circus ring and its spangled backdrop where silvery letters proclaim: "Royal Lichtenstein Circus—World's Smallest Circus—1/4 Ring!"

The Workers set up a table and begin to ladle out lemonade and hand out bags of popcorn. The children and the old men line up meekly for their share, and soon the air is filled with sounds of munching and rattling paper. Then from behind the backdrop a creature of fantasy steps into the ring—a mime in classical whiteface with a small, elegant goatee and a bald head fringed in long reddish hair, clad in white tights and a stiff tunic in brilliant primary colors. "Ladies and gentlemen!" he cries in a hearty voice, "The show is about to begin! Please come forward and be seated! The upholstery leaves something to desire, but with air conditioning like this, who can complain?" Gazing hungrily, the people step closer like sleepwalkers and sit down quietly, making room for the children in the front.

A shrill whistle blast, a burst of circus music, and out come three others dressed alike into the hustle-bustle of the magic ring—they scurry about, tumbling, colliding, in the time-honored manner of clowns. They wobble about on unicycles, make things appear and disappear. A prop cannon is wheeled out, and little girls shriek and cover their ears as a match is applied to the bung hole— and out hops a poodle in a little red jacket to parade absurdly about on his hind legs. A pair of pigeons appear in a box that was empty but an instant before. And now, a quiet moment as one of the clowns mimes the story of a bird who gave away his golden wings. This is a bit fey for a battered wino, who comes to the edge of the ring holding out a pair of high-heeled shoes, to raucous laughter from his buddies. A Catholic Worker dissuades him gently. The show goes on: a skit about Sally Sweetheart and a pickpocket proves more to their taste. Sally, played by a lanky youth with a curly mop of hair and greasepaint granny glasses, is befuddled when the red and orange and purple scarves that cover her parasol miraculously appear in her purse. The audience is entranced at a teetering tightrope-walker; an old man stares openmouthed, his paper-bag-covered wine bottle clutched forgotten by his side. The whistle blows, and more animals are brought out—a cat that leaps through a hoop of fire, a woolly monkey in a little apron who drinks greedily from a soft-drink can and runs casually along the high wire, and at last a delicious little horse who soberly circles the ring with two of his dainty hoofs atop the curbing. And even a wild animal—a large gray-flannel stage elephant who tap-dances blowsily. The bearded mime lights two torches, and as he throws back his head and lowers the flame into his mouth, a grinning man from the audience steps up to have his cigarette lit. The ancient vaudeville turn about the one-dollar bill that pays off everybody's two-dollar debts is as funny and baffling as ever. At last the grand finale—all four mimes fill the air with flying white rings. As they juggle they recite a rhyme in Spanish ("Otra vez!" cries a matron in the back) and suddenly flip the rings over so that they are blue—and then red—and then green in a whirling storm of color. Gasps, and applause, and cheers. They come forward together, and in an oddly formal and literary moment hold the audience quiet with a poem of tribute to the circus and to joy.

Afterward, as the mothers lead the little ones away chattering excitedly in Spanish, as the old women gather up their shopping bags, a tall black man in a shabby jacket calls out, "Hey, Bill, how'd you like it?" His snaggle-toothed friend lights a cigarette and looks up with a face newly touched with wonder. "Well," he says cautiously (for life has dealt him more than his share of disappointments), "it was better than I thought it would be."

There were traces of white greasepaint in Nick Weber's reddish eyebrows as we sat down to coffee after the show. "Somebody told me you used to be a Jesuit priest—" I began. "I *am* a Jesuit priest," he answered quickly.

"What? And you spend all your time traveling as a street performer? Do you have to justify that to anybody?"

"I wouldn't," he countered firmly. "And if I had to, I'd just say that who I am needs to be a priest, needs to be a clown." The Jesuits were founded to be flexible, he explained, and from the first they dispensed with traditions and were willing to experiment. In Europe the order has a long history of involvement with the theater; they popularized ballet, invented stage machinery. "But I didn't start doing what I'm doing because I developed a theology for it. Quite the reverse."

Nick saw his first circus when he was a little boy in 1945. "I never recovered. The magic of bringing a whole city and setting it up and making all these things happen, and then disappearing at night—that's just been the biggest phantasm in my life." In 1957 he entered the Jesuit order, took a master's degree in theater, and developed his own theater groups. "Eventually I came to see it as much too precious a format," even though he was using conventional scripts to provoke unconventional discussion with the audience. "The people there already cared about art or literature. I needed a format for the ordinary guy, wherever he might be." So in the spring of 1971 he took a box of props and went out to a busy corner in San Jose "just to see if I could handle an open-ended crowd. I did mime, fire-eating, juggling, magic." Nick very quickly found he had a following among the old people in the downtown hotels. "They came up and forced me to take money, even though I didn't want it." Nick's full-time commitment to street theater was a gradual transition. "One day I came home to the University of Santa Clara where I was stationed and I had a bear and a dog and a monkey . . ." He realized he had become a circus. The show grew, and he performed in shopping malls, on college campuses, and in churches. "As I moved into circus, my heart was not repressed anymore. It was saving my life as an artist. I followed my heart, not my intellect." The next summer he assembled a troupe—Steven Aveson (later of the Shakespeare Brothers), a girl and a boy, and a duck ("You get a lot of mileage with a duck")—and hit the road. "I'd eat fire every time the crowd got thin, and sometimes I had to do it ten times a day." They got a few bookings, and gradually built a circuit for what became the Royal Lichtenstein Circus.

For the last nine years he has traveled the same route: from Seattle he turns east, crosses the northern United States in the winter as far as Washington, D.C., then returns through the Midwest to California and up the coast to his home base in San Jose. For eight months of the year he is on the road; the other four are spent putting together the next show. Nick and his three current fellow-performers—Stephen Coyle, Larry Ryan, and Philip Wellford—travel in one amazingly small truck, in which everything is precisely stowed. The little vehicle has racks and hooks for rigging and props, and food and space for four humans, two dogs, a cat, two pigeons, and a horse.

Nick readily admits that he has made a life commitment and feels in touch with all the past performers who have been part of the tradition. He gestured to the glaring concrete outside the window. "The street is so ugly. When you walk down the street, there's nothing rich and soft. The performing arts truck with the spiritual." He leaned forward earnestly. "God and art are utterly useless. Any time you try to make them useful you prostitute them. Art is something that renders profound truths irresistible. What goes on here" (he waved toward the circus ring) "that is godly or divine is a chance for people in dull or overstructured environments to play. We 'make believe'— an exercise of faith. If people do that, their chances of meeting the Big Surprise are heightened. If you don't welcome surprise, if you don't welcome the possibility that one thing can instantly turn into another, that this could be more than what meets the eye, or the ear, or the senses, then the chances that you're going to meet the transcendent are minimal, as they have become for those who limit God to a certain time of the week or a certain kind of architecture."

The solemn moment had ended. He settled back and smiled. "This comes home to me like a boomerang whenever there's a breakdown on the truck. It's a hell of a hard task to see the Holy Spirit in a broken axle."

The Royal Lichtenstein Circus was the only show I had seen on the street that used animals extensively. I wondered why. Nick explained the near-prohibitive regulations imposed on animal trainers. The Animal Welfare Act requires a federally issued license for permission to show cats and dogs. It is inexpensive, but inspectors follow up by arriving at unexpected intervals to check cage-size, ventilation, and other details of the animal's environment. Exotic creatures are regulated by the Fish and Game Bureau. "Their rules depart from all the traditions we've had in transporting and training animals," he said. The Humane Society and the Friends of Animals don't really understand the facts of animal training and are suspicious of trainers, Nick claimed. For instance, an inspector might object to the absence of a water tub for an elephant during the day. Yet any trainer knows that elephants are watered thoroughly twice a day only, and if the empty tub is left the elephant will pick it up with her trunk and throw it.

Whitney Brown and his dog Brownie have been one of the very few trained dog acts on the street, although it was always debatable whether Whitney or Brownie was the trained member of the show. The comedy revolved around Brownie's apparent reluctance to do any of his tricks and Whitney's increasing frustration with his obstreperousness. Brownie retired to a farm in Vermont in the spring of 1980, but tales of his personality linger among buskers. His stubbornness about performing was more real than feigned, and on one occasion Whitney decided to show him who was boss. They had been traveling with a small circus and Brownie had figured out that he was safe from Whitney's wrath whenever an audience was watching. Sneakily, Whitney arranged for a fake audience made up of roustabouts and other performers to assemble before showtime one morning. Brownie, feeling smug and secure, balked at his first trick, and Whitney descended on him with well-earned punishment. Ever after that, he was always a bit unsure that an audience was genuine. He loved drawing a crowd, however, because he didn't have to do anything but sit peacefully with a visored cap pulled down over his shaggy brows and a pipe clenched in his muzzle. Passing the hat was also one of his favorite moments; he and Whitney would go down among the crowd and while Whitney collected money Brownie would collect bones from the doggie bags of the tourists who had just had dinner. "It was sort of a primeval thing, you know," said Whitney. "A dog and his master going hunting. He really dug it."

A few buskers, like Richard Wexler or H. P. Lovecraft, have worked their dogs into the acts, and an occasional cat lover attempts to make a living with those animals. "All you can do with cats is augment the natural patterns," said Nick of his sleek feline jumper. Roland McGriff draws a crowd in Central Park with a cat-train: tricycles and toy wagons linked together with four smug Persian cats as passengers. Puff, Omar, Tiki, and Sebrina blink sleepily and respond only occasionally to their owner's commands to roll over or sit up. More accomplished are the three kitties belonging to Leo the Catman in Westwood Village. Leo discovered the possibilities of cat-busking one traumatic day when he had been evicted from his apartment in Hollywood. As he sat penniless on the sidewalk, surrounded by his few belongings, some passersby stopped to admire his tiger kitten. Leo had taught him to stand on his hind legs and embrace a dollar bill with his front paws. He told them about the trick and was startled when the people pulled out dollars for the cat to take. The money-making implications dawned on him; he went to the pound and got two more cats, and spent every waking minute training them. He is emphatic about the difficulty of teaching tricks to cats: "Lady, *you* go home and try to teach *your* cat to do this," he said, nodding his head. Satin-black Wizard, a Siamese, shakes hands on request; snow-white Fairy holds a spoon and eats from it; and little yellow Psychic does his dollar-bill hug. All three depress a bird-shaped lever on a little box to release fortunes rolled in narrow pellets. Leo rewards each trick immediately with a morsel of food on a tiny spoon.

THE CANDY DANCER

"I smell taffy," says my nephew as we climb the hill at the Renaissance Faire. "There it is." I point—a little metal cart on wheels with three steaming wells. A young man with the delicate bone structure of the Southeast Asian takes a slim wooden stick from a bundle, scoops out a handful of golden taffy, and shapes it onto the end of the spike. Circling and swooping in a serene dance of creation, his hands flutter over the lump of pliable candy, coaxing out a curving wing, pulling out threads of an-tennae or feelers, shaping a snaky tail to coil around the long wooden handle. Clippers hidden in his palm feather the edges of wings or create tiny claws. In a moment or two an airy fantasy beast has appeared atop the stick in place of the shapeless mass. With a flourish he presents it to a wide-eyed child in the ring of spectators. Such a creature of magic could never be sold, only given away to the innocent. But a jar on the cart is crammed with dollar bills presented in almost shamefaced tribute.

"Dream Fantasy," said the candy dancer's card; his name is Masaji Terasawa and his real avocation is riding horses cross-country. Several other unclassifiable acts I encoun-tered only by anecdote or hearsay: Jason Serenas, the classical whistler; Raymond Chance, who offers "music with knives"; and the Oily Scarf Wino Band, whose lead player makes music on a xylophone made up of bedpans in graduated sizes. But the people I really regretted not seeing were the trio in Philadelphia who come out in the street in lederhosen and alpenstocks and climb the side-walk as if it were vertical.

There is also a whole category of people who bridge the gap between performer and vendor—those who sell services of some sort. Fortune-tellers and palmists and tarot readers and I Ching interpreters and horoscope analyzers are often seen in a lively street scene, set up at little folding tables or hawking from the open doors of vans. Face painters are nostalgic leftovers from the psychedelic sixties and do a roaring business in New Orleans just before Mardi Gras. Back massages are a marketable talent, and even foot rubs. Caricaturists and portrait artists are really merchants, but the person who draws in chalk on the sidewalk comes from an older European pattern. Backgammon lessons are sometimes offered on the spot, and I have even seen a chessmaster who revealed his boredom with amateurs in his price scale: "Lessons $3, challenge game $5."

And a Note on Dance

Being a dancer myself, I was disappointed to find that dancing buskers are almost nonexistent. The one significant exception is found in the black street-dance tradition of New Orleans. Small boys in that city will tap-dance to whatever music is available: the sounds of a band through the open doors of a café, their own singing, or the music of another street performer. One of the best is Robert Williams, who has learned to involve the audience by teaching some simple steps to a volunteer. Clyde Holmes, known as Porkchop, is an elderly survivor of the long history of New Orleans street dance. Diminutive and dapper in a plaid sports coat, he taps with astonishing precision and energy for a man of seventy-seven, and ends his routine with some spectacular acrobatic slides. Another elderly New Orleans street dancer is Willie-When-He-

Walks, who is a "strutter"; Willie can only occasionally be seen doing his odd choreographed walk down Bourbon Street.

Dance sometimes appears as part of an act. Mountain Mime incorporates the talents of belly dancing Jeanne. Charlie Cox clogs and bucks as a visual addition to his banjo playing. He finds that "the more motion I make, the more money I make." He lays down a little square of rug on the asphalt to protect his feet; "this stuff eats up the bottoms of shoes like you wouldn't believe." Irish and old-time American bands draw bigger crowds with a step-dancer as part of the performance. Lisa Gray is a fourteen-year-old gamine who sings songs from the movies of the forties and dances in period style between the verses. I heard rumors and caught glimpses of other acts: a Kabuki dancer had been seen in the middle of the (dry) fountain in Washington Square; a male ballet dancer had broken his leg when he leaped on the cobbles in front of St. Luke's Cathedral in New Orleans; a belly dancer named Jenya Hacobian had just left town when I was in San Francisco.

Patty Lovecraft, wife of Harry, evolved her tap-dancing street persona to consciously desexualize her performance. As Sister Mary San Andreas of the First Church of Science Fiction, she is protected by her habit. "She's a real unorthodox nun," says Patty. Sister Mary usually taps a cappella on a sheet of Plexiglas for resonance and resilience. "Dancing on concrete really makes your feet hurt," was her explanation. Often she is joined by three others, because the augmented sound of a group effort is much more effective. Together they have made an annual exploit of the Labor Day Long Distance Tap Event—two miles down Market Street, tapping every step of the way.

Dance draws spontaneous amateur performance like no other art. If the rhythm of a band is infectious, there will soon be dancing going on—at the edges of the circle, in the middle of the circle, then everywhere within hearing, everybody bouncing and clapping. Venice Beach has had a number of dancing semibuskers. They do it for the joy, and if coins come their way, that's extra. Modern-day bacchantes, their names are legend: Gypsy Rosa, Regina the Snake Lady, Sexy Brenda, Houda the Belly Dancer, the Soular Sisters.

BACCHANTES ON THE BEACH

Up and down the beach the word spreads: "The Soular Sisters are coming out! The Soular Sisters are coming out!"

"No shit, man? Hey, I gotta see this!" Sunbathers gather up their towels; bicyclists unlock their wheels from lampposts; old men in tarnished suit jackets rise stiffly from park benches; strollers meet friends, get the word, change direction to hurry along the Oceanfront Walk toward a spot where three musicians are tuning up, ignoring the expectant crowd that has ringed them at a respectful distance. They lean casually against the sun-brilliant white stucco wall behind a satin-draped stand on which "The Soular Sisters" is spelled out in glitter. We find a good vantage point and climb up on a bench to see over the heads.

"Where are they? When are they coming out?"

"They're in their apartment getting high—they'll be out when they feel good enough," says a wizened little man, squinting his eye to look up at me against the sun. He points to the stucco building across the walk.

Everywhere people are drinking from paper bags hid-ing beer cans; the little grocery store down the block is doing a brisk business. A shimmer of the cymbals, and the musicians begin a wandering, atonal modern jazz sound. They find each other; the rhythm solidifies; the percussion begins to cook—and the Soular Sisters run out into the black asphalt space and fill it with their presence, leaping, shaking, whirling in a pink and purple and yellow flurry of ribbons and feathers. The crowd yells encouragement. It is plain that the sisters have had no formal dance training, but they move with natural athletic grace and enormous sensuality, arching their backs and contracting into pelvic thrusts, gyrating their hips from wide-planted feet. In the costumes with yellow-feathered ankle-wreaths, skirts of flying ribbons through which their tanned thighs gleam, they seem to be pagan priestesses, but when I look more closely at the faces beneath the clouds of curly pale brown hair I see ordinary-American prettiness, strong young bodies that might be more at home in gym shorts.

"Go, Lilly! Go, Rose!" screams a sandy-bearded man on a bicycle.

"Which is which?" I ask the little man below me.

"I dunno—I never can tell," he shrugs. "I hear the guy they live with can't tell either." He points to a well-dressed man in his thirties who stands quietly to one side taking pictures with an expensive camera. "They say he buys their costumes and everything."

The music has built to a frenzy. The sisters turn cartwheels, one arches back to the ground to make a bridge, her hair falling over smooth shoulders, her taut belly straining up while her sister writhes under her. The crowd is clapping in rhythm now. Lilly and Rose unfasten the ribboned skirts, whirl them overhead, and dance in the shiny pink-purple leotards that leave their muscled thighs bare almost to the waist. Their bodies gleam with sweat, and the clouds of hair have become damp ringlets clinging to their foreheads and necks. The taller sister dances up to a man in the front row, vibrating her flat belly and satin crotch. Her eyes are vacant, glazed, and her mouth hangs loosely. The crowd screams, jumps up and down, whistles its approval. On and on they dance, beyond exhaustion, beyond words and reason and time. Then suddenly they are gone.

A sigh of release from the audience. The musicians gather up their instruments, pass the hat perfunctorily. Slowly, people mount their bicycles, throw away empty beer cans, pick up their beach towels. A fluffy yellow feather blows across the walk, and a man picks it up, tucks it in his pocket as he walks away through the thinning crowd.

WORKING THE STREET

"The street's a good school. That's where you get your diploma in singing. You see the audience—it's there in front of you, touching you. You hear its heart beating and it says what it thinks. You know what pleases it, what it doesn't like. And if it cries now and then, the take'll be good."—Edith Piaf, in *Piaf,* by Simone Berteaut

Perceptive buskers are often almost mystical about the energy flow between audience and performer. The television-oriented American public often resists that crucial involvement. "Whenever people form a circle, they always do it so the widest part of it is right in front of us," says dulcimer player Doug Berch. "It's hard to get them to come in. They want to keep that invisible fourth wall. A lot of people will go on the sides because they don't want you to look directly at them, or that way they figure they can stand there for a long time and they don't have to put money in." Involvement is important, says Will the Juggler, because "otherwise they're just watching TV. They can look you right in the eye like a piece of meat, shrug, and walk off. If they look at me and I look back and we have eye contact, we're gonna have an exchange. I force them to it. I've got people mad rather than let them be bored."

Breaking the fourth wall is necessary to keep people from falling into their television-viewing attitude—inert, not reacting aloud or rewarding the performer. Bringing a spectator into the act is the most common device for creating involvement. A magician or a juggler will ask a volunteer to hold something or participate in a trick; a mime will assign roles in the fantasy world he or she is creating. The rest of the audience identifies with that person, and through that identification comes to the realization that this show is truly live, and that they have their part to play.

Because a street performer gets immediate feedback from the audience, there is never any doubt which parts of the act are good. If the spectators are not pleased, they vote with their feet. If they *are* pleased, the performer is instantly rewarded with laughter, applause, and money. "The audience writes your act," says Harry Lovecraft. "You do any silly thing out there, and if they seem to like it, you leave it in." "So the longer a person is on the street, the more effective the act becomes?" I asked. "Perhaps," said Harry. "It certainly does tend to vulcanize the whole thing."

I had wondered if a busker's intimate connection with coaxing money from the crowd might influence the performance toward money-producing gimmickry rather than toward excellence. Butch Mudbone had lamented, "If I play some of the stuff I like—if I play the old Delta stuff, they dissipate." Is a crowd-pleasing act necessarily a good act? Paul Levey sees this as a dichotomy of skills: "It's important to be good with your music, but it has absolutely nothing to do with professionalism. You learn what jokes you can use and can't use and how to run your tunes together. You can be Cole Porter and get on the street and not make a dime. You've got to learn how to work the crowd."

Some street performers are truly artists, but they adjust their performance to the demands of the audience when they have to make their rent. Phoenix tells how it goes: "The only time I play for money is when I need it. I'll play a solo that will just knock people's heads off, then I'll take my hat and just ask them for money—right now, right while they're clapping. And that will always bring a rush of money. But I'd rather not hustle the people. In the close proximity of the commercial and the artistic on the street there is a certain brutalization, a soiling of the spirit." But he reflected, "Even in a club your music has to make the cash register jingle." I had noticed that classical guitarist Don Gribble usually opened a set with "The Entertainer," a piece that got enthusiastic response. Was he ever tempted to move the rest of his repertoire in that direction? I asked. He claimed not, but his reason was revealing: "A classier repertoire gets a classier take."

In the long view, a truly great performer of any kind has to have both a close awareness of the audience's reactions and a dedication to the art for its own sake. The give and take of the street can be growth-producing up to a certain point of competence, and limiting beyond that. "A lot of excellent street people learn how to work the crowd and never increase their range. They use the same juggling act; they eat the same fire; they do the same jokes; they make a good living, and then that's it," says Paul Levey.

The street is self-corrective, and a performer who refuses to learn its lessons doesn't last long. But even a brief appearance by such incompetent would-be buskers damages the fragile public acceptance of street performing. Barcelona Red voices anger at their crude insensitivity: "A lot of people think 'Let's go to New Orleans and play in the streets,' and they just grab a guitar and they don't know how to play and they get out there and bang away. They say (hoarsely) 'Why don't ya give me some money, man! Shit!' They're not musicians. They're not performers. They're just bums!"

Some additional advice for novice buskers from experienced hands who are concerned about protecting the image of street entertainment: "Try to keep clean and well-groomed even on the road. Use the hot water in McDonald's restroom if you have to. We feel it's important to look as pleasant as you can so people are not frightened of you. Put on a pair of shoes; look nice! Don't sing the shabby blues. That's why people kick you away!" says Allegra. Busking etiquette requires that performers keep a distance from each other. The first person to arrive at a good spot gets it, although some older buskers will claim territorial rights over a favorite location. In some cities performers are expected to relinquish a prime spot after an hour or so to make room for others. There is an etiquette to jamming, too; permission must be asked and granted to sit in, and the newcomer must not expect to share the hat unless it is offered. A sign to prop against the guitar case or the hat lets the audience know the name of the performer they're watching and can also drop a hint about donations. Finally, business cards with a local phone number are essential for follow-up on requests to perform at parties and weddings and clubs.

Solo women performers have special problems. Unfair as it is, in our culture a woman alone making herself conspicuous in the streets is seen as advertising her sexuality. Like so many other aspects of busking, this is a tradition going back to the Middle Ages. John Towsen observes in his book *Clowns:* "While there were many female jongleurs, they were handicapped by being regarded as no better than common prostitutes, and were accordingly harassed by civil and religious authorities." Patty Lovecraft finds little difference in modern attitudes: "They think that a woman, no matter how strong you are, is weak and cannot stand on her own on the street and take care of herself—which is really untrue. They look at you, and there you are, a woman by yourself, trying to deal with an audience and trying to get them to give you something, and it just doesn't work as well as a man doing it. But when you put more than one woman together, they have a totally different attitude toward it." Another form of protection, as we have seen, is the androgynous mask of the mime or the asexual image of the clown. Donna Israel, who plays Irish concertina on Fifth and Sixth avenues and on the Staten Island Ferry, finds that a good ploy is simply to pretend not to understand sexual approaches. Donna, who usually wears jeans and stands over six feet tall, feels that image and bearing are important: "If you go in on the same basis as men, then people take you on the same level."

LISA LEARNING

"Just call me Sandman Simms, Jr.," says Lisa Gray, hooking her thumbs in her rainbow suspenders and throwing back her shoulders in the oversize glen plaid sports coat that hangs almost to her knees. Lisa is fourteen, and for a year she has been serving her apprenticeship on the open mike at Sarno's Restaurant in Hollywood. Now she is taking her renditions of forties movie songs to the streets on Venice Beach. This is her third Sunday as a street performer, and she is learning the techniques as she goes. "Boy, this is a rough audience, I'm telling ya!" she says cheerfully.

Lisa Gray dances on the Oceanfront Walk

We walk along the beach looking for a good spot,
Lisa, and Debra, her mother, and I. Debra carries a
shopping bag with the big tape player, a thermos of
water, extra costume pieces. "That might be a good spot
up ahead," points Lisa, but when we get there a guitarist
has staked out the territory. The next space is dominated

by a blaring radio, and the one after that feels dead. At last she finds a place she likes; Debra turns up the taped piano accompaniment, and without any preliminaries Lisa steps into the center of the walk clutching a battered felt hat and begins to belt out "Toot, toot, tootsie! (Goodbye)," with Al Jolson gestures. On the chorus she dances, a high-stepping, elbow-pumping delight, a mischievous gamine in striped socks and rolled-up orange pants parodying a vaudeville hoofer. A crowd has gathered, caught by her good big voice and well-rehearsed professionalism, but as soon as the song is ended they clap and move on, ignoring the hat she has put out. "Uh, folks, here's my hat!" she calls after them, but it doesn't work. "Leave a hat down all the time," we tell her. "You've got to hold them for at least three songs before they'll feel like putting money in." She nods, concentrating and preoccupied.

We move on. The next spot goes better. She does "Tootsie" again, "Somebody Stole My Gal," and then "Lydia the Tattooed Lady" ("Lydia, oh Lydia, that encyclopedia . . ."), wiggling her hips in Groucho Marx mock-sexy gestures. Between songs she tries to hold the crowd by talking, in spite of being out of breath: "The next number is about a lady I know who's quite amazing . . . ," and they stay for the whole set, and leave a couple of dollars and change in the hat.

Several photographers have been shooting, and one man with a videotape camera has just left. Lisa runs after him but comes back chagrined. "All he'd say was 'Arrivederci,' " she says. "I guess he's from Italy. Last week some guy from a Brazilian TV station taped my whole act. I'm going to be famous all over the world before I make it here!"

She takes a drink from the thermos, hitches up her pants, and steps out to sing again. Debra has noticed that it gets a laugh when Lisa throws "If you don't get a letter then you'll know I'm in jail" to a man in the audience, so this time she tries several other lines, working in close to the people. It does get laughs, but when she turns her back to the other side of the circle, her voice is hidden and the crowd there immediately begins to drift away. We discuss it afterward. "You'll have to get the circle smaller, ask people to move in," says Debra.

"Tell them 'My pickpockets are only working the third row,'" I suggest, lifting a line from the Shakespeare Brothers. The next time she tries it. The act gets better; she keeps the energy high; her crowd control is visibly improving. Afterward I give her a hug. "You're a real trouper. Thanks for letting me come along and watch."

"Hey, it was fun!" she beams. Her voice is not the least bit hoarse from three hours at top volume.

On the way back to the car we pass Slavin' David and the band. They are playing "Rock around the Clock." Lisa jumps out in a knock-kneed Little Richard dance, draws whistles and cheers. When the song ends she thanks Slavin' and digs down in her baggy pants to pull out some of her own street change to leave in his guitar case.

After the crowd has been assembled and entertained, then comes the crucial moment—the pitch (or the "audience-disappearing act," as performers call it among themselves). A clever and profitable pitch has to be timed and worded just right. It must blend with the exhilaration of the applause for the finale and use that goodwill; a five-second drop in the energy at that decisive peak can leave the performer with an empty hat. It must let the spectators know that the busker is in the streets to make a living, not for idle amusement. And it must leave them laughing and feeling good about themselves for choosing to reward the performer.

Ira the Mime introduces "my financial partner, the bucket. I do all the work; he takes all the money." Moonbeam observes, "Applause is the performer's butter—but I could sure use the bread." After the Juggler is more oblique: "We'd like to remind you that because of the local ordinances we can't ask you for money, so when we're through, just throw it right in here." Ray Jason invites people on the upper balconies to throw change down into the hat, but explains that to avoid injury in case of a miss it should be wrapped in a dollar bill. Butterfly announces that "for those of you who are new to San Francisco, the average donation here at Pier 39 is five dollars. ('Course I haven't had an average for quite a while now . . .)"

David and Roselyn integrate their pitch with the last chorus of their pickup tune, "Tryin' to Make a Livin'." Roselyn says, "Now some of you folks seem a little bit shy, so tell you what I'll do, I'm gonna pass on by." And she hands around the rhumba box while David finishes the song. Stingy contributors earn her disdain: "Keep the dime, honey. You should always keep a dime in case you get busted."

The Fantasy Jugglers never ask for money. Dario describes their technique: "At the end Lana just spins the bucket on her finger and sets it down and opens her arms, and people come and put in like they know what they're supposed to do." Gentle Allegra make no pitch either. "We feel that we are giving our music away freely, and if people feel moved to give back, okay."

Just how much money do buskers make? To the observer, a hat brimful of dollars looks like a lot of cash, just by the sheer physical presence of the green and silver.

Somehow it seems more real than the oblong of cardboard with numbers on it that most workers take home on Friday. But that hat may only hold twenty or thirty dollars—not a lot compared to that conventional paycheck. A related fallacy is the multiplication game: "Let's see, if he made thirty dollars for this twenty-minute show, he gets sixty dollars an hour, and that's (eight times sixty)—Wow! $480 a day! And (five times $480)—$2,400 a week!" This is nonsense. It is not physically or emotionally possible for performers to give of themselves eight hours a day, five days a week. Even four hours of performance is draining, and not all of those shows will be top earning quality, nor will they be continuous. Crowds and locations vary, and the busker's energy rises and falls during the day. In most cities street performing is limited to certain months of the year, certain days of the week, certain times of the day. And the vagaries of the weather and the police wipe out even some of those few good hours. So the truth is that very, very few full-time street performers make more than $3,000 a year. Many of them, as we have seen, supplement their income with other forms of show business, or the reverse—they are able to survive in show business because of their street earnings. Perhaps less than a fourth of all serious buskers in America are actually making a living off their hats. And that, as Roselyn says wryly, "depends on what you call a living."

That quarter the vacationing businessman tosses in the hat so casually, then, is important to the busker—for both financial and emotional reasons. The money in the hat is personal tribute for the performer, an assurance that he or she is valued. "When you're putting yourself out there, *you* are on the line," says Stu Buck. "I can't understand how someone can stand in an audience, watch something for fifteen minutes, and then walk away," puzzles mandolin player David Corina. "They'll clap; they'll ask for tunes; they'll take our goddamn picture; they'll ask questions—and then nothing." Stu speculates on the reasons for this lack of generosity: "Maybe they don't know any better. Or they're too cheap—everybody wants something for nothing, a free show. Or they might think you're doing it for fun; they don't see the performer as a person who has to pay the rent." Whatever the cause, noncontributing audiences baffle and anger buskers. Slavin' David speaks out of his pain: "Like you could have a hundred people around you and they all clap and everything, and they all enjoy the show and they don't give shit. It hurts my feelings, 'cause I got a lotta pride and I'm very proud of what I do—a little bit sensitive and overly emotional at times, and I feel like I'm being used. It ticks me off."

But a performer whose audience fills the hat to overflowing reaps more than money. Lovecraft glows as he describes the feeling: "Every coin comes with a compliment. If they're going to take the time to come up and put a dollar in the hat, they're saying, 'You're worth a hell of a lot more. I really enjoyed that. Not only did I stay to watch it, but I'm going to be irrational, totally irrational, and throw away a dollar.' It's a nice way to live, to know that you're living on love."

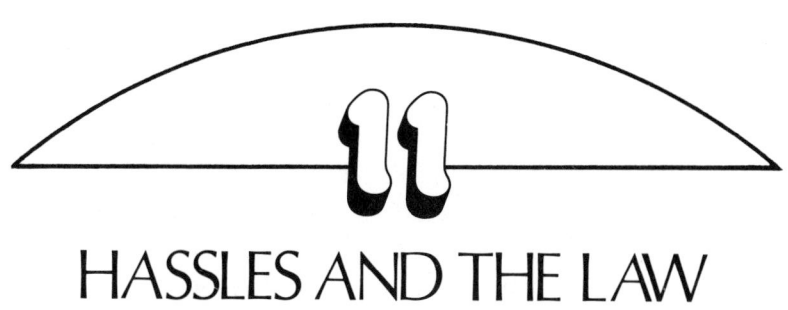

HASSLES AND THE LAW

"Mankind are greater gainers by suffering each other to live as seems good to themselves, than by compelling each to live as seems good to the rest."

—John Stuart Mill

Working in the public streets, buskers are wide open to danger. They are subject to hassles from both ends of the spectrum of respectability. Madmen and criminals—those crazed by life or drugs—have at them. Shopkeepers blame them for empty cash registers. And the police, who should offer equal protection, are often their enemies. The law gives them no recognition or shelter. But recently some landmark legal decisions have pointed the way to a new acceptance of street performing as an inherent right of free expression.

The street performer's joy is the closeness to the audience, the directness of the unshielded contact between entertainer and entertained. But that very openness leaves the busker a vulnerable and conspicuous target for less pleasant contacts with drunks, junkies, and crazies. Society's flotsam and jetsam is adrift in the streets, and these confused and angry derelicts are often attracted by the islands of warmth and laughter around the performer. Their behavior can range from heckling or muddled attempts to join the show to actual life-threatening attacks. Nearly every performer told me a hassle story or two.

Such incidents are difficult tests of a busker's ability to deal with the unexpected, to improvise solutions to a potentially disastrous moment, and to keep the sympathy of the audience. Sometimes the best that can be done is not very good: Jim Cappe was once grabbed around the legs by an intoxicated girl as he sped past on his unicycle; he could do nothing but break his fall. Gentle Edie the dulcimer player tries to preserve the theatrical illusion for protection: "One time a drunk came up and sat down next to me on the steps and spilled his wine all over my hat. I was so mad! But you know what the thing was? If I had kept my cool, the people that were standing around listening would have been able to show their disgust, but I was so disgusted myself that I scared them away. I realized then that I had to keep my cool and be tolerant with drunks myself. If other people want to be disgusted or yell at them, okay. But it wasn't my place, because I was on the stage."

A mismanaged confrontation with a drunk can lead to police involvement and loss of rapport with the audience. One night in Westwood, Jingles and Frank were accosted by a wino who lurched into them, ground out a cigarette in the guitar case, and then spit on it. That confrontation ended with the arrival of five patrol cars. Puppeteer Gary Schnell had a bad experience with a drunk who tried to grab Milton the Puppet and pushed the stage so that the microphone cut Gary's lip. "It was the only time I ever stopped the show," he said ruefully. He lost his temper, came out of the puppet theater, and shoved the man, who fell backward and hit his head. The police came and took the drunk away. "It was really awful," said Gary. "I got back in the stage, but you could feel it from the crowd; they didn't leave; they just waited for Milton to come back up and say something. The best he could do was, 'Oh well, what would you have done if he came into your office?' But it was no good." Even without a confrontation drunks sometimes come between a performer and the audience. Harry Anderson remembers "sometimes I'd finish my act and pass the hat and some drunk would jump up and slobber 'Give the kid some fucking money!' and everybody would leave; I wouldn't make a cent."

———————————————————————•———————————————————————

SLAVIN' DAVID HANDLES A DRUNK

The band has just segued from their usual driving rock-abilly beat to a slow, sneaking blues. The beach sun is hot, and so is Slavin' David. A grizzled, bone-thin dere-lict staggers into the center of the circle, clutching a nearly empty bottle of muscatel, stretches out on the asphalt, and peacefully passes out before a hundred spectators. His hands are folded on his chest and his whiskery chin points up to the sky. David, who in his childhood on Venice Beach has seen everything, plays on. Into the circle dances a slight bearded black man, also a bit sozzled around the edges. Undulating with the slow sensuous beat, he takes off his sunglasses and bending over the oblivious wino he places them on his nose and adjusts the earpieces carefully. Next, with all the coyness of an expert stripper, he unbuttons his plaid sports jacket and approaches the sleeper on tiptoes,

225

swiveling his hips gracefully and holding the coat out delicately like a matador challenging the bull. Solicitously he covers the unconscious form, tucking in the edges with exquisite care. Then the shirt, which he folds and slides under the lolling head for a pillow. The crowd is entranced, but Slavin' David, beginning to feel that this is getting to be too much of a good thing, ends the piece and opens his mouth to cope. But the dancer is not through with his victim—leaning over him with a glass of water he cajoles, "Look, Bob, vodka! Open up!" and dribbles a few drops into the half-open mouth. The wino rouses and splutters indignantly, "W'er y'doin'?" David, sensing that in another instant the situation will no longer be amusing, calls out, "Hey, Bob, you're spoiling my act! Get him out of there, somebody! You guys, get him up and lean him against the wall over there! Come on, Bob, you can hold up the wall while you listen to the music!" The old man is helped up and half-carried to the wall, and another volunteer carries over his precious wine bottle. The dancer greets a friend and walks away down the beach. David picks up the beat and the group is off into another song. The crowd joins in, clapping and laughing, the moment forgotten, and behind them old Bob dozes off in the sun.

Sometimes even skilled attempts to head off aberrant behavior can backfire. Gary Schnell tells another story: "One time on Market Street a guy came up, leaned into the stage looking at Milton, and said, 'Kiss my ass!' He kept doing it, kept on saying it, and I couldn't get him to leave. I tried all kinds of little funny things to get the guy to move along and nothing worked. So Milton finally said, 'All right! If I kiss your ass, will you leave?'

"He said, 'Yeah!' So I said (trying to call his bluff), 'Okay, drop your pants!'

"Well, right there in downtown San Francisco, with all these tourists watching, this guy took all his clothes off and stood there and mooned Milton. I was crouching inside going 'Yii!' "

Other stories of unbalanced actions are not so amusing. Harry Anderson pointed to a scar: "This is a street happening—my broken jaw. Punched in the mouth by a drunk on the street. He shattered, absolutely shattered my jaw. Another time on stage at the Cannery I had a newly killed bird thrown in my face from the balcony." Mime Jim Moore was performing in front of the New York Public Library, according to *Village Voice* columnist Howard Smith, when a man he had never seen before in his life came racing through the crowd, ran up to him, and punched him in the nose, knocking him down. Jim got up, finished his act, and passed the hat. As he was passing it he saw the man still in the crowd, purple-faced and seething. So he backed off and said, "Why did you do that to me? I don't know you!" The madman said, "But *I* know *you!* You're my ex-wife's lover!"

Tightrope-walker Bruce Smith was attacked by an assailant with no reason at all. Bruce was practicing on the wire in Central Park when "a big lummox shook the rope so that I fell off, and then he beat me to a pulp and put me in a hospital." Bruce is stoic about the assault. "You have to pay your dues, I guess," he shrugs. Even a master busker like steel pianist Victor Brady is not immune to violence. The tall, impressive black man was robbed once at knife-point of all the money he had taken in, but a second time, even though the robber had a gun, Brady used his street skills to talk him out of it. In spite of such ever-present hazards I talked to no performer who carried a weapon or protection other than a whistle or (in one case

only) Mace. Those who earn their living in the streets cannot afford to admit fear of them.

A more benign annoyance are the street evangelists
who regard the busker's crowd as a ready-made audience
for their own proselytizing. The Hare Krishna people are
especially persistent about taking over a performer's space,
and even, I was told, have plainclothes bouncers who run
interference for the saffron-robed chanters. Individual religious fanatics are more easily dissuaded, and a clever
busker can even work them into the act. On the Florida
State campus Moonbeam was interrupted as he juggled
fire by a Jesus person who, to the crowd's amusement,
pointed with a trembling finger and cried out, "Sorcerer!
You like to play with fire—you'll spend eternity in
flames!" At the Mardi Gras, where evangelists are numerous, the Water Street Boys Jug Band coped nicely with a
preacher who stepped into their circle to harangue. The
leader gestured to the band, who struck up a waltz; the
trombone player laid down his instrument, seized the
preacher around the waist, and danced him around and
around until he stamped off with his dignity in shreds.

Stuffy members of the establishment, too, can sometimes be kidded out of authoritarian attitudes. A third
anecdote from Gary Schnell illustrates. He and Milton
were performing outside Royce Hall on the UCLA campus
when the Dean of Student Activities came up to Milton
and said, "You can't do this!"

"What? Who are you?" said Milton in furry-faced
surprise.

"I'm the Dean!"

"Well, what are you talking to a puppet for? What kind
of a stature is that for a Dean?" The man spluttered helplessly, and Milton took advantage. "Okay, Dean, sit down
over there and let me finish my show!" And he did.

Even those who would seem to have common cause

with street performers can be the source of hassles. A puzzling antagonism is that between street vendors and buskers. It would seem that they should be a coalition, but in no city have the two kinds of street people made alliance, with the one exception of a brief period in San Francisco when the vendors were agitating for a license structure. The performers joined in the political campaign for that objective, but never benefited from it, and a residue of bitterness was left. Suggs remembers, from her days on the vendor-lined sidewalk, "You were always dealing with this creepy feeling at the back of your neck." Everywhere performers feel a tinge of envy at the vendors' relative security. "They can put their umbrellas out there, camp out there from dawn to sunset," said Scotty. Vendors, on the other hand, perceive themselves as one shaky rung up the capitalist ladder and resent the buskers' freedom. "It looked to me like the performers were having more fun," said Will the Juggler of his days as a Renaissance Faire peddler. Whatever the reasons, it is not uncommon for a vendor to call the police when the size of a crowd or the loudness of a performance affects the sales pitch.

However, the buskers' most serious enemy is the shopkeeper. In this antagonism, society's disapproval is acted out. Performers blame the merchants for initiating police harassment, and there is often direct evidence of the truth of this accusation. To the objective observer it is odd that businesspeople should be so opposed to street entertainment. It seems axiomatic that performers draw crowds to a shopping area and put everybody in a happy mood to spend. The bits of change that go into the buskers' hats only prime the pump for further purchases rather than deplete the shoppers' wallets so that they go home empty-handed. But merchants don't agree. Allegra said, "They feel a dollar put in the case is not going to buy a knickknack. The shop owners have visions of us making tons of money. They get upset because they pay taxes and we don't." The truth is that very few street performers make enough money to file for income tax.

Scotty Hill attributes the antagonism to envy. "They're just jealous because we can walk out on a sunny day, set up, make our money, and bam, we're gone. We don't have any sidewalks to sweep; we don't have any shop to lock up; we don't have to worry about our shop catching on fire. . . . When they see that, they're angry. They don't see the hard times we have sometimes."

This attraction/repulsion is manifested in what Harry Lovecraft calls the Hassle Cycle: "If the shop owners are having a bad time and not making enough sales that day, they'll see a big crowd out watching a street performer and they'll say, 'Now if those people weren't watching his show they'd be in my shop.' So then they'll get the street performer arrested, but their business will not improve, and there won't even be the people outside the place. Then the shop owners will get together and say, 'We ought to get some entertainment or something in here,' and they'll ask us to all come back again. They usually change their minds about two or three times per season."

A few wise merchants understand the symbiotic relationship of performer and shopkeeper. The Cambridge Businessmen's Association is friendly to performers, an attitude that developed only gradually over the years as it became increasingly obvious that the huge and lucrative evening crowds in Harvard Square had come primarily to see the show. An occasional merchant or café owner in other cities will invite a busker to set up in front of the shop, or even offer a haven in a recessed doorway. But it is far more typical for shopkeepers to define street entertainment as a situation to be "cleaned up"—at least on alternate months.

This schizophrenic attitude can be intensely frustrating for a performer. Doublethink is evident not only in the Hassle Cycle but in the discrepancy between civic public relations and the actions of the cop on the beat. Scotty Hill sent copies of an August 1979 *Time* Magazine article lauding street musicians to the mayor and the council of New Orleans and got "a beautiful response saying it was good for the city." Yet only a few months later police were arresting performers at random every night on Bourbon Street. Paul Dion and Marc Wiener were the targets for an even more striking example of civic schizophrenia. They must constantly battle with the police to keep their spot at the foot of the Metropolitan Museum steps. "We've been told several times never to perform here ever again. 'Get out of this spot—it's not yours!' But we keep coming back. We've had summonses to come to court; we've been to court . . ." Yet in the winter of 1979 they were given an award by the City Planning Commission for making the streets of New York a better place. The very next week "the police came and said, 'All right, Paul, I don't want to see you here ever again.' " Frustrated beyond endurance, Paul ran home and got his award and went to the police station. He thrust it across the desk and cried, "Here! Look!" They were unimpressed.

The conversation of street performers is studded with references to police and arrests. The stories range from accounts of remarkable kindness to accounts of remarkable brutality. Police can be sympathetic and appreciative of a good performance, or they can be apologetic at having to carry out a complaint registered by an upstairs tenant or a shopkeeper, or they can be brusque and disapproving, or they can be brutal and even psychotic. The busker can never be sure what to expect from the local cops, even from one night to another. They are completely subject to the vagaries of the individual policeman and must submit without recourse, even though they suspect that surely their rights are being violated. Concertina player David Wyman speaks this helplessness: "Me, on the street, the Man has the badge and the gun. He may not be right, but I'll do what he says." The cop is the ultimate theater critic for the busker.

Sometimes the harassment takes the form of minor interference. Musicians might be forbidden to use amplifiers in certain spots, or after certain hours—but the rules are subject to change without warning. Once in a while props and equipment will be confiscated: fourteen-year-old juggler David Gregory was relieved of his knives one afternoon because he was "under age"; the Human Jukebox has been trashed twice—once in a garbage compactor.

Barcelona Red conveys the performer's anxiety with erratic police behavior as he describes Bourbon Street when the heat is on: "The police get the word to bug everybody. So they're telling 'em, 'Well, it's against the law to play on the street after eight o'clock—or after ten o'clock—' Every cop has his own way of harassing, so you don't really know what the story is."

Such petty harassment can sometimes escalate into city-wide sweeps in which every performer in sight is hauled off for a night in jail. Paul Levey describes a San Francisco event in 1978 that buskers remember as Bust Day: "The city started cracking down because there were so many street musicians and they didn't know how to bust the bad ones and the winos and the guys smoking dope and keep the good ones. The police didn't know who the people with the reputations were—only Herb Caen and the people who write about it knew. So they were just picking up everybody on the streets and throwing them in the paddy wagon. We all got bopped." Their band, the Bourbon Street Irregulars, had just been loaded aboard the Black Maria when leader John Stafford came around the corner.

While he stood distraught on the curb, the wagon pulled away as the band waved from the tailgate and launched into a mournful rendition of "Prisoner of Love."

Imprisonment is hard on the free spirit of street performers. Roselyn Lionhart shudders at the thought. "When I'm in jail, I just pace up and down, up and down. That's all I do. I wore out a pair of shoes once in two and a half days in jail. And jail food—wuh! You can't eat jail food!" Magician Harry Lovecraft uses magical tricks to distract a cop bent on arrest ("Police are like animals—they react to fear") but occasionally he, too, spends a night in jail. "They put me in a cell next to an open window, and I could have picked the lock with a coat hanger or a safety pin and escaped—but you get shot for escaping."

The basis for all this patternless and unpredictable torment is that busking is not illegal but extralegal. Nowhere does the law say that a person may not perform on the street, nor does the law usually admit that a person *may* perform on the street within certain limits. This lack of legal status leaves busking open to interpretation as begging, obstructing traffic, or disturbing the peace. Often there is not even this much attempt at legal grounds for harassment. It simply strikes the cop on the beat as behavior that is outside the scope of what normal law-abiding people ought to be doing on the streets. If a performer *is* arrested, his offense is usually not given the dignity of a trial; he will often be treated like a minor nuisance, locked up with drunks and prostitutes, and released the next morning with charges dropped.

The time-honored American response to harassment and suppression is to organize, and street performers when pushed beyond their normal hassle-tolerance sometimes do attempt to join forces to bargain for better working conditions. San Francisco pianist John Timothy drew together a group to protest the arrests in that city in 1978:

"It looked like the police were really cracking down, so I had a meeting and a lot of people came to it. There were five of us elected and we went and talked to the local police captain; things mellowed out."

Boston performers put together a loose organization in the same year to debate scheduling procedures with the management of Quincy Market. In Los Angeles in 1977, Jingles and David and Roselyn organized the short-lived but grandiosely titled International Street Performers' Association to open up the streets of Westwood. And the buskers of New Orleans, through their sense of community identity, an informal grapevine, and occasional meetings, have been able to work from time to time with a team of volunteer lawyers.

But such attempts at organization are short-lived and usually fade away as soon as the immediate crisis improves. Street performers are by nature individualists and do not easily fit into the self-effacement of group action. Although performers speak wistfully of their desire for protection from the police, the very idea of organization goes against the grain with them. A structured association is equated with regulation and loss of freedom. Paul Levey declared with passion, "If you're happy with no one telling you when you have to work, then why do you want to join an organization that says you have to be here at nine o'clock to get your spot? You're organizing a thing that's based on nonorganization!"

Legalization of street performing on the civic level means licensing, another form of regulation that buskers view with suspicion. San Franciscans often describe their street vendors' plight as an example of the destructive results of licensing: Several years ago the sidewalk artisans organized and lobbied for the city to legalize them; now their spots are assigned by lottery and there is a three-year wait for an artist who wants a permit. Even worse, they have been taken over by merchandisers and stand after stand sells only fake "handcrafted" goods from Taiwan. It is true that the streetsinger's license in Boston has had the beneficial effect of freeing performers from police hassles, but that structure is often honored by buskers only in the breach. In the few other cities where licensing exists, performers usually regard the red tape involved in getting a permit as an avoidable irritation, a nuisance, to be ignored if possible. After all, one reason they are in the streets is to escape such bureaucratic requirements.

———————————————•———————————————

POTLUCK IN JACKSON SQUARE PARK

Johnny Light believes in organization, believes with a mystical intensity that if the good people can only all get together, then the world will be all right. So today he has called the New Orleans street folks to a meeting in the park to talk about their common distress—why have the police been cracking down this week? Blossom is here, with his red rubber nose, and gaunt, whitefaced Ira in his purple tux. Two-thirds of Allegra is present— Anna's skirts spread wide around her as she leans on Jack's shoulder. Edie in her motley, little Beppo, big genial Don Hill, a ragged young juggler, dozens of musicians with their worn guitar and fiddle cases laid carefully aside on the grass. In the midst of the group is a collection of food offered by those who have money today—a bag of potato chips, a bunch of bananas, a package of cookies.... They are pleased with themselves

235

for having a meeting, but as tentative and awkward in their unaccustomed formal togetherness as forest animals at a waterhole.

"Who's been hassled this week?" asks Johnny. "Put your name down on this clipboard—our lawyer wants to have a list."

Blossom is telling his story: "A cop grabbed me and said, 'Would you mind coming with us?' "

"Just out of a clear blue sky? Just out of nowheresville?" marvels Stu Buck.

"If anyone gets busted for street music, we should all get together and throw a benefit for whatever it takes. This could be a political model; we need to know that we have somebody in a camaraderie!" says the juggler expansively, carried away by the occasion.

"Yeah, but who should the one phone call be to?" says Ira, bringing it down to earth. "Who has a phone and fifty dollars?" There is general rueful laughter.

Johnny is ready with practical advice. "I have a phone number for our street lawyer here. Now let me suggest that you only use this number when arrested—don't call her up and ask for the time of day or anything."

The talk turns to conjecture on the reasons for their persecution. They are genuinely baffled, and a little hurt, that they should reap so much hostility for enlivening the streets with their talents.

"They think we're all riffraff!" cries a fiddler. "Beethoven, he started playing on the street!" Everybody names famous musicians who got their start on the street. "Bob Dylan got kicked out of town here!"

"The Bourbon Street Merchants' Association feels that every nickel we make comes out of their personal pockets," says Stu. Heads nod. "And the thing is, even if they have an agreement with us, and there's no law, we're only playing at their largesse."

"What about the guidelines they put out last year?" asks Edie. "Who's got a copy? Read them out loud."

Johnny pulls out a creased mimeographed sheet. "The musicians will police themselves and take responsibility for moving on when a crowd blocks the sidewalk . . . musicians will not use amplifiers . . . musicians will not play in front of the St. Louis Cathedral during services . . ." There are murmurs of "I don't think there's any violation of those on our part . . . except for amplification, maybe . . . and blocking the sidewalk—but you can usually tell your people to move over . . ."

Don Hill has a suggestion. "We need to educate people. Like our own commercial: 'We do this for a living! Support street music!' "

"Or a permit system, maybe," offers a guitarist. They discuss this for a moment, but the consensus is opposed. "The reason we're street performers is that we don't want to have a career; we don't want to have someone telling us what to do. And I don't want to have someone telling me where I can play. Besides, you could have a really great performer come to town for two days, and if he didn't have a permit he couldn't work and everybody would miss out on him."

Johnny seizes the moment to point out the moral. "There's a friendly network of artisans, all over the world, and we're all connected whether we know it or not!"

The talk drifts to solutions—publicity, TV coverage, buying a page in the newspaper—but it is plain that they are becoming confused and overwhelmed. Johnny the good organizer sets a date for the next meeting and adjourns; the food is passed around. Across the park, at a safe distance, some tourists take pictures while the buskers share their picnic.

STREET MUSICIANS' GUIDELINES

At a meeting on March 29, 1979, between representatives of the City of New Orleans and over 50 street musicians, the following agreement was reached:

1. In general, street music is acceptable in the French Quarter as long as the music is not too loud and the streets and sidewalks are not blocked.

2. The police have been requested to equitably enforce the noise ordinance.

3. The police have been requested to assist by asking crowds to disperse when they block the street or sidewalk.

4. The musicians will police themselves and take responsibility for moving on when a crowd blocks the sidewalks; the musicians shall ask onlookers to cooperate in keeping the sidewalks and mall areas clear for access to shops and the artists around Jackson Square.

5. Musicians will not use amplifiers or play steel drums.

6. Musicians will not play in front of the St. Louis Cathedral during services. Careful attention and cooperation is particularly requested here.

What is needed, it should be apparent, is an overarching federal court decision sanctioning street performing as a legal activity. But a trial case is necessary for such an action, and until recently buskers have not had the persistence, courage, and money to battle to establish their rights. Scotty Hill, himself the subject of an arrest in New Orleans that led to the banning of street music on Royal Street for more than a year, said: "We haven't been crusading and standing our ground, which we could do— even take it to the Supreme Court, maybe, if we had the energy. But then we'd end up spending our lives in court rather than playing music, and I think life's too short."

In 1977 fiddler Ron Bowman decided life was *not* too short to fight for justice. After he and two others—singer Cynthia Jones and guitarist Matthew Allen—had been arrested in New Orleans once too often, they approached the American Civil Liberties Union for help in setting up a class action suit. The ACLU declined on the grounds that they could not possibly win, but private attorney William Rittenberg was willing to take the case. He and attorney Mary Howell in June 1977 filed for an injunction (District Court of the United States for the Eastern District of Louisiana, #77-1872, Bowman v. Landrieu). In their brief they linked First Amendment rights of free speech with street performing, citing a number of precedents establishing that the Supreme Court "has extended the First Amendment . . . to cover a broad variety of symbolic expressions and has clearly mandated that this symbolic expression is given the full range of protection and guarantee as is provided for 'pure speech.' . . . The Court has clearly indicated that it considers artistic forms of expression to be fully and unqualifiedly given the same protection as any other form of expression." Furthermore, whether or not the expression is done for money is irrelevant; streets and sidewalks are presumed to be appropriate places for First Amendment activities. In their resounding conclusion they point out that "at stake here is not only the fundamental constitutional guarantee of artistic, political, cultural and social expression, but also the protection of an entire heritage of oral and musical expression which is uniquely a part of the rich history of the City of New Orleans."

During the six months the suit was in progress several other buskers were arrested and their cases were handled by Rittenberg and Howell. Elderly and famous tap dancer Porkchop was arrested for "begging" on Bourbon Street and charges were dropped five days later. Raymond Chance ("Music with Knives") was not so lucky: he was charged with "carrying a concealed weapon" and spent twenty days in jail. German mime Maria Ramer was arrested in October as she sat on the steps of the Cabildo in Jackson Square; police had warned her not to collect money for her performance, but an eager spectator insisted on dropping seventy-five cents in her tip can, which cost her her freedom. Howell and Rittenberg used her case to write a brief that attempted to clarify the distinction between begging and busking. Since Maria's English was minimal, they planned for her to give her testimony in mime, and arranged to have it videotaped in court for the record. In the meantime, Ron Bowman's case reached a favorable conclusion, and because Maria's visa was about to expire, a compromise was negotiated by the lawyers in December. Ron agreed not to pursue his suit further if charges were dropped against Maria and if the French Quarter merchants unofficially acknowledged the rights of street performers. Unfortunately, the judge in Bowman v. Landrieu, R. Blake West, died before his written opinion could be published, and so no firm precedent was established. Two years later nightly arrests were again a commonplace. Mary Howell (now of Howell,

Kellogg, and Bayer) continues to take occasional busking cases, although she claims that she would rather not have legal regulation but prefers negotiation and compromise. Like the performers, she fears that legislation would bring control and possible suppression.

Control was the issue in the most recent and most important busking lawsuit: District Court of the United States for the District of Massachusetts, #79-1455-Z, Goldstein v. Nantucket. The decision in this case will undoubtedly be the precedent-setter for street performing adjudication for years to come, and it has already begun to change the status of busking in other cities. The suit was initiated by Robb Goldstein, the Nantucket Troubadour, with the help of Boston ACLU attorney John Reinstein. Robb's flaming red beard and hammer dulcimer are a common sight not only in his native Nantucket but all up and down the Eastern Seaboard. Judge D. J. Zobel, in his Memorandum of Decision, describes him sympathetically: "Plaintiff has for many years studied and performed the traditional music of Nantucket and is an acknowledged authority on the music and folklore of the island. He plays a number of instruments from the hammer dulcimer to the fife and banjo and he sings. He has performed the music of Nantucket at numerous festivals and in concert but prefers to perform in the tradition of balladeers, on the street. When he performs in Nantucket, he customarily plays the hammer dulcimer and sings, and positions his open dulcimer case so that passersby may contribute donations, and some do."

Robb, however, had been prevented from doing just that in his own town for several years, even though he had applied for a special permit to do so. At last, in 1978, he was told that street entertainment was regulated by the Transient Vendor Bylaw, which imposed licensing criteria of (1) financial responsibility of the applicant, (2) effect on neighboring properties, and (3) the opinion of town merchants. Robb bridled at these, especially the last, and filed suit on the grounds that his First Amendment rights were being denied. Judge Zobel agreed, and in his Memorandum of Decision in September 1979 he stated clearly and firmly that street music, even though it is *commercial* "speech," is protected by the Constitutional guarantee of freedom of expression, and therefore is not subject to narrow regulation by municipalities. And most specifically, "the requirement of merchants' approval is irreconcilable with freedom of expression. It is unqualified censorship and it is just what the First Amendment forbids."

The precedent is clear. In other cities performers are finding that a few well-chosen sentences from Goldstein v. Nantucket are enough to bring even the most intractable city managers around to sweet reasonableness. It remains only for a case to be carried to the United States Supreme Court to establish the principle strongly for the whole nation, and to free buskers everywhere to perform in peace.

What then, is the meaning for American society to be found in the renaissance of busking? In one sense, it is a symptom of a rebirth of confidence in the possibilities of cities. For a time in the sixties it seemed as if middle-class America was on the point of abandoning the urban environment to the forces of despair and crime. With the return of life to the city has come a willingness to see the street as a happy place—and the busker is indicative of this change of mood.

In another sense, street performing can be seen as having the aesthetic function of providing a training ground for artists and entertainers. Not since the death of vaudeville has there been a place for performers to serve an apprenticeship. Little theater and open mikes provide the audience but not the living. There is no other place but the street to practice that electric, growth-producing interchange with a crowd and to be free to devote one's whole energy to it without being forced to earn the privilege by typing or washing dishes. Perhaps one reason television is so bad is that it gives the entertainer no corrective—or worse, a delayed and distorted corrective. On the street, as in the old days of vaudeville, a performer can test and polish and refine an act until it is a thing of confident perfection.

But the deepest significance of the phenomenon of busking for America lies in our attitude toward work. The Puritan ethic has decreed that one must work to be an accepted member of society. Work has been defined as that which one has to do, and play as that which one wants to do. For work to be fun was a contradiction. And the reason for work was not just to have access to food and shelter but to accumulate the material goods by which a person's worth was measured. Buskers have chosen to live outside this framework of attitudes. They own little and want nothing more, and they follow their own inclinations and enjoy their lives in leisurely ways that are allowed to only the richest and most successful of those who climb the capitalist ladder. From the lives that we have seen in these pages it should be apparent that street performers are not dropouts or rejects from society. They are people who have chosen to step out of the American dream into their own dream.

AFTERWORD

Contemporary street theater can be viewed in the larger perspective as a new form. Entertainment institutions have lifespans—they live or die or evolve. Street performing is in its infant stage—it is developing. It can mature and spread all across America. The United States is ripe for this movement. It can be viewed as a sign of hope in a society plagued by a multitude of problems: consumerism, bigness, greed, energy waste, distrust, impersonalness, despair, disparity of wealth. It's not going to topple the system, but combined with other private, personal and heartfelt commitments it can have a tremendous impact.

In recent years I have been visited often by a recurring dream. It is a very lucid, beguiling vision and I think that it deserves to become a reality. In that dream barren concrete sidewalks blossom forth with happiness, enchantment and brotherhood. So get out there and go for it!

RAY JASON,
San Francisco
(In *The Next Whole Earth Catalog,* 1980, and *California Living,* July 11, 1976)

REFERENCES

Articles

ANDRIOTAKIS, PAM. "Business Is at a Standstill for Curtis Read and That's Just How He Likes It." *People* Magazine, November 6, 1978.

ASEN, SCOTT. "Brother, Can You Spare a Dime?" *Pictorial Living,* August 1, 1976. [Stephen Baird]

"The Bands of Summer." *Time* Magazine, August 27, 1979, pp. 66–67.

BRANTON, MICHAEL. "For Love and Money." *Berkeley Monthly,* February, 1980, pp. 22–23.

BROOKS, PATRICIA. "Reflections of a Mover and a Shaker." *American Way,* September 1979, pp. 93–96. [Rouse Development Company]

"Comic and Queer Old Ordinances." *The New York Times,* July 1, 1923, Section 7, p. 10.

References

DRAKE, SYLVIE. "Marceau: Sculptor of Space." *Los Angeles Times,* March 27, 1980, Part VI, pp. 1, 4–5.

GARLINGTON, PHIL. "Laureate of Street Takes Bitter, Sweet." *Los Angeles Times,* June 9, 1978. [Pagan the Poet]

GRALLA, PRESTON. "All the Street's a Stage." *Boston Globe,* August 13, 1978. [Stephen Baird]

HUFFMAN, ROBERT M. "An Analysis of Street Juggling." Unpublished paper, 1979.

JASON, RAY. "The Joys of Street Performing." *The Co-Evolution Quarterly,* No. 20, Winter 1978/79, pp. 56–60.

JOHNSTON, STEVE. "Street Sounds." *The Seattle Times,* December 2, 1979, Section A, p. 3.

KLAICH, MICHELE. "Ticket to the Streets." *Air California* Magazine, August 1979, pp. 40–43. [Ray Jason]

"Hurdy-Gurdy Fees Abolished by Mayor." *The New York Times,* March 8, 1935, p. 23.

LATTIN, DON. "City's Juggler Home After a World Tour." *San Francisco Sunday Examiner & Chronicle,* April 20, 1980, Section A, p. 10. [Ray Jason]

MANNA, SAL. "Street Stars." *L.A. Reader,* November 30, 1979.

"One-Man Band on Broadway." *The New York Times,* August 28, 1927.

PETIT, PHILIPPE, and REDDY, JOHN. "Two Towers, I Walk." *Reader's Digest,* April, 1975, pp. 204–27.

PETIT, PHILIPPE. "The Vagabond Theater." *The Village Voice,* July 2, 1979, p. 58.

PRENDIVILLE, JULIE. "The Serious Side of Clowning Around." *Los Angeles Times,* August 1, 1980, Part VI, p. 12.

ROSENTHAL, DAVID N. "Around-the-world Juggle by a Bay Street Artist." *San Francisco Independent and Gazette,* August 27, 1979, p. 13. [Ray Jason]

STEIN, RUTHE. "Now They Come Marching In(doors)." *San Fran-*

References

cisco *Chronicle*, August 7, 1979, p. 16. [John Stafford and Paul Levey]

Sweet William. "X Swami X, the Sidewalk Comic." *Los Angeles Times*, Calendar Section, December 23, 1979, pp. 70–71.

Books

Berteaut, Simone. *Piaf: a Biography*. Harper, 1972.

Boyle, Wickham. *On the Streets; A Guide to New York City's Buskers*. New York City Department of Cultural Affairs, 1978.

Chambers, Edmund K. *The Mediaeval Stage*. Oxford University Press, 1903.

Davis, R. G. *The San Francisco Mime Troupe: The First Ten Years*. Ramparts Press, 1975.

Dittrich, Rudolf. *Juggling Made Easy*. Stirling, 1963.

Grove's Dictionary of Music and Musicians. Fifth ed. St. Martin's Press, 1954.

Lesnick, Henry, ed. *Guerrilla Street Theatre*. Avon, 1973.

McKechnie, Samuel. *Popular Entertainments Through the Ages*. Stokes, n.d.

McNamara, Brooks. *Step Right Up*. Doubleday, 1976.

Sanders, Toby. *How to Be a Compleat Clown*. Stein and Day, 1978.

Scholes, Percy A. *The Oxford Companion to Music*. Oxford University Press, 1938.

Sheridan, Jeff, and Claflin, Edward. *Street Magic*. Doubleday, 1977.

Towsen, John H. *Clowns*. Hawthorn, 1976.

Weisman, John. *Guerrilla Theater*. Anchor, 1973.

Willeford, William. *The Fool and His Scepter: A Study in Clowns and Jesters and Their Audience*. Northwestern University Press, 1969.

APPENDIX

National Associations and Other Contact Points

Magic:
Society of American Magicians
66 Marked Tree Road
Needham, MA 02192
(617) 444-8095
Herbert D. Downs, International Secretary

Magic Castle (magicians' club)
7001 Franklin Ave.
Los Angeles, CA 90028
(213) 851-3313

Mime:
National Mime Week
Los Angeles Mime Guild
6253 Hollywood Blvd., Suite 312
Los Angeles, CA 90028

(213) 463-1404
(213) 242-9136

Dell' arte School of Mime and Comedy
(Carlo Manzzone-Clementi)
Box 816
Blue Lake, CA 95525

Celebration Mime Theater
(Tony Montanaro)
Box 44, RTD 1
South Paris, ME 04281

Clowns:
Ringling Bros. and Barnum & Bailey Clown College
P.O. Box 1528
Venice, FL 33595

Fred (Garbo) Garver and Bob Berkey's Clownshop
c/o Joan Sand
130 Pine St., #2
Portland, ME 04101

Juggling:
International Jugglers' Association Newsletter
Bill Giduz
P.O. Box 443
Davidson, NC 28036

Acrobatics:
U.S. Sport Acrobatics Association
P.O. Box 7
Santa Monica, CA 90406
(213) 394-0949

Igor's Acrobatic World (esp. hand-balancing)
(Igor Ashkinazi)
1111 Lake, #54
Metairie, LA 70005

Music:
Banjo Newsletter (bluegrass)

Box 364
Greensboro, MD 21639

Country Music Association
Music Circle North
Nashville, TN 37203
(615) 244-2840

American Oldtime Fiddlers' Association
6141 Morrill Ave.
Lincoln, NB 68507

Eagle Tavern (old-time music)
355 W. 14th
New York, NY 10014
(212) 924-0275
(212) 929-9827

Dulcimer Players News
Madeline MacNeil, ed. and pub.
Box 157
Front Royal, VA 22630

Street performers' newsletter and advice about college-campus busking:
Stephen Baird
Box 570
Cambridge, MA 02138

INDEX

253

Index

Index

Index

Index

Index

Index

Index

About the Author

Patricia J. Campbell is known among street performers as the Boswell of busking. Her interest in sidewalk entertainers stems from her own experiences as a belly dancer at street fairs and festivals. To research *Passing the Hat* she visited and traveled with buskers for a year and a half and did hundreds of taped interviews. She is a young-adult library specialist and teaches adolescent literature at UCLA. She is also the author of *Sex Education Books for Young Adults, 1892–1979*. She lives at the beach near Venice, California.

About the Photographer

Alice Belkin was graduated from the University of California at Berkeley and Smith College School for Social Work in Northampton, Massachusetts. She works as a psychotherapist in Los Angeles when she is not on the road as a photographer.

"Taking pictures of street performers has special problems," says Ms. Belkin. "In addition to cold feet, jostling, crowds, poor light, and no control of the weather or of the staging, there are problems like being unable to use flash with jugglers because the afterimage seems to create an extra ball in the air."